Thinking Black

Thinking Black

William Cooper and the Australian Aborigines' League

Bain Attwood and Andrew Markus

Aboriginal Studies Press

First published in 2004 by Aboriginal Studies Press, Australian Institute of Aboriginal and Torres Strait Islander Studies (AIATSIS), GPO Box 553, Canberra ACT 2601.

This publication is copyright. Apart from any fair dealing for the purpose of private study, research, criticism or review as permitted under the *Copyright Act 1968* and subsequent amendments, no part of this publication may be reproduced, stored in a retrieval system or transmitted in any form or by any means, electronic, mechanical, photocopying, recording or otherwise without prior written permission.

Text © Bain Attwood and Andrew Markus 2004

National Library of Australia Cataloguing-in-publication data:

Attwood, Bain.
Thinking Black: William Cooper and the Australian Aborigines' League
Bibliography.
Includes index.
ISBN 0 85575 459 1.

1. Cooper, William, 1861–1941. 2. Australian Aborigines League. 3. Aborigines, Australian - Social conditions. 4. Aborigines, Australian - Government relations. 5. Australia - Race relations - Sources. I. Markus, Andrew. II. Title

Front cover illustration: 'Barmah Forest', Lin Onus 1994. © Lin Onus, Licensed by VISCOPY, Australia, 2004

Back cover photograph: Lin Onus and Gary Foley holding Australian Aborigines' League banner, 1996. Banner created by Bill Onus *c.* 1950. Photograph by David Langsam, Foley Collection.

Frontispiece: William Cooper, 1861–1941 (courtesy Alick Jackomos)

Foreword

I am very pleased to have been given the opportunity to say a few words about my grandfather, William Cooper.

In the year 1929, as a very small child, I was taken by my mother, Amy, to live with my elderly grandfather, William Cooper, and his wife, Sarah. They were known to us grandchildren as Puppa and Nan. They lived in a timber/corrugated iron house lined with hessian. Puppa had built this shelter on the banks of the Murray River, two miles down from the Barmah Township, opposite the Cummeragunja Aboriginal Settlement. We lived there for about four years.

My grandfather then decided to move to Melbourne to further his work in fighting for the rights of our Aboriginal people, for better conditions and standards for our people. There were many Aboriginal issues he fought for. He was mainly self-educated and his main aim in life was the equal treatment of the Aboriginal people. His move to the city would make his fight a much easier task, as there was support from others that had a passion to achieve the same results as he did.

I later joined my grandfather and three other grandchildren. We lived in Footscray. Times became harder as Puppa was now of pension age. Because of money being scarce his fight for the fair treatment of Aboriginal people became more difficult to continue and achieve, as there were times when Puppa could not even afford a train fare. Many times I remember him walking into the city and back to attend meetings and voice opinions to anyone who would meet with him to listen.

There were also many meetings held at Puppa's house. I can still remember the faces of the people who came to those meetings. Puppa would sit and write letter after letter to get his point across. There were times I remember him sitting on cold days with a blanket around him as there was no heating in the house.

After a while I returned with my mother to Mooroopna. Sometime later Puppa and Nan came back to the country, as they were both getting on in years and Puppa's health was starting to fail. In 1941 he became ill and was admitted to the Mooroopna hospital where he peacefully passed away. He was buried at the Cummeragunja cemetery.

My grandfather's passion, and his sincere hard work, determination and dedication to help change conditions for Aboriginal people are things I will never forget. It was amazing. He never gave up and continued to fight to make life better for his people. His hard work has come a long way as I believe that all his struggles over those years with meetings, letters and simply his presence have made life for our people today a lot easier. He was dearly loved by his family and the Aboriginal people and he has earned the respect of the wider community.

Alfred Turner
April 2003

Contents

Foreword	v
Acknowledgements and note on the documents	viii
Abbreviations	x
Introduction	1
Documents	25
Notes	130
Sources for documents	135
Bibliography	137
Index	141

Illustrations *between pages 86–87*

Agnes Cooper and children, c. 1900
William Cooper to Rev. Ernest Gribble, 16 July 1933
Some residents of Cumeroogunga church, c. 1914
William Cooper at Framlingham
William Cooper to H. Makin, 19 March 1934
The choir sings, April 1936
Day of Mourning, 26 January 1938
William Cooper to Thomas Paterson, 25 June 1937
Notice, Day of Mourning, December 1937
Church of Christ Sunday School, Cumeroogunga, c. 1938
Supporters of the Cumeroogunga walk-off, c. March 1939

Acknowledgements and note on the documents

Research for this book has been conducted in many libraries and archives over the last two decades, and we are grateful for the assistance provided by librarians and archivists over this time at State Records New South Wales; Australian Institute of Aboriginal and Torres Strait Islander Studies; Centre for Australian Indigenous Studies, Monash University; Matheson Library, Monash University; Mitchell Library, State Library of New South Wales; Mortlock Library, State Library of South Australia; National Archives of Australia (Canberra and Melbourne); Noel Butlin Archives Centre, Australian National University; Public Record Office Victoria; State Records Office of Western Australia; Rhodes House Library, Oxford University; Royal Historical Society of Victoria; Screensound (Melbourne); State Library of Victoria; State Records of South Australia; and the University of Sydney Archives.

The research was funded by the Australian Research Council and the Faculty of Arts at Monash University. Verity Archer provided research assistance, and scanned and word-processed the documents.

The late Mr Gillison Cooper and the late Mrs Sally Russell encouraged Andrew Markus's earlier research, and granted permission to reproduce letters written by their father. The Jackomos family gave permission to reproduce photographs from Alick Jackomos's collection. We are indebted to the estate of Lin Onus for permission to reproduce his painting *Barmah Forest*.

The royalties from the sale of this book will be donated to the Centre for Australian Indigenous Studies at Monash University for the purpose of funding the biennial William Cooper Memorial Lecture, which was established in 2001.

The documents, drawn from libraries and archives throughout Australia as well as overseas (as listed at the end of the book), have been arranged chronologically and have been reproduced with their original spelling and punctuation, except where there were typographical errors in typewritten material. Words and punctuation have been inserted in square brackets where we thought it necessary to clarify meaning. Square brackets around ellipses indicate these were in the original document. The documents are referred to throughout the introduction in bold text, thus: (**1**).

Abbreviations

AAL	Australian Aborigines' League
AIATSIS	Australian Institute of Aboriginal and Torres Strait Islander Studies
APNR	Association for the Protection of Native Races
ASS	Anti-Slavery Society
CRS	Commonwealth Record Series
NAA	National Archives of Australia
PROVic	Public Records Office Victoria
SASA	South Australian State Archives (now State Records of South Australia)
SRNSW	State Records New South Wales

Introduction

William Cooper was the founder and leader of the Australian Aborigines' League, the most important of the first crop of Aboriginal political organisations formed in Australia. In the 1920s and 1930s other bodies were founded in settled Australia, principally the Australian Aboriginal Progressive Association, the Native Union and the Aborigines Progressive Association. However, these were short-lived and had a narrower focus than Cooper's League.

Not surprisingly, perhaps, Cooper has long been remembered by his own people, often called the Yorta Yorta, but he has only returned to the notice of other Australians quite recently.[1] In the late 1970s the anthropologist and historian Diane Barwick prepared an entry for the *Australian Dictionary of Biography*, which was based on ethnographic and historical research she had first conducted among Cooper's kin in Melbourne in the early 1960s; and in the mid-1980s Andrew Markus published a selection of Cooper's numerous letters to government, which he had collected in the course of doing archival research for a study of Commonwealth policy in the 1920s and 1930s.[2] Since then, historians have increasingly focused their attention on the agency and perspectives of Aboriginal people. Both Cooper and the League have attracted more attention; additional historical records have been found; and historiographical debate has ensued, mostly regarding the nature of the rights demanded by or for Aborigines.[3]

Despite this, Cooper is still unknown outside a very small circle of people. This is unfortunate to say the least. As this volume of historical documents will amply testify, Cooper is a significant historical figure, a leader whose distinctive political programme presented a considerable challenge to governments in the past and continues to resonate strongly today. As such, he deserves a wider audience among both Aboriginal and non-Aboriginal Australians.

Life story

Information about William Cooper before he came to political prominence in the early 1930s is sketchy. Often all we can do is imagine his life by reconstructing the broader historical circumstances in which he lived. (In Australia there were no oral history projects like those conducted among former slaves in the United States in the 1930s, and the written record yields comparatively little.) Only recently have historians discovered his date of birth.

Cooper was born in his people's country on the junction of the Murray and Goulburn rivers on 18 December 1861. He was the fifth of eight children of a union between a white labourer, James Cooper, and a Yorta Yorta woman, Kitty Lewis. By this time the Yorta Yorta had been thoroughly dispossessed, following a pastoral invasion of their territory in the mid-1830s. One of Cooper's earliest memories was of his mother calling out to her children that 'white man coming' and their 'dart[ing] into hiding until the terror passed'. Like other indigenous groups in Australia, Cooper's people were decimated as a consequence of European colonisation, dying from white men's violence and diseases, though Cooper claimed that as a boy he had witnessed a meeting of several hundred Yorta Yorta men.[4]

Following clashes between the white newcomers and the local landowners, many Yorta Yorta worked on pastoral properties in the area. These included Moira and Ulupna stations, owned by a prominent businessman and politician, Sir John O'Shanassy. When Cooper was seven years old, O'Shanassy took him to Camberwell, a suburb of Melbourne, where he lived as a member of O'Shanassy's family for three years or so. He was then sent home to the Murray to work as a hand on Moira station, where he learned horse-breaking and other rural labouring skills.

Around this time Cooper's mother and some of his brothers and sisters settled at Maloga, a mission station that Daniel and Janet Matthews had established on the banks of the Murray River near Echuca after they began evangelising among Aboriginal people in the area in 1866. Cooper soon joined them. In August 1874 Matthews noted in his diary: 'The boy, Billy Cooper, shows great aptitude for learning.' By 1876 Cooper had apparently decided he wanted to stay on Maloga, telling the missionary: 'There couldn't be a better place than this.' A few years later, though, Cooper and two of his brothers, Bob and Jack, moved to another mission station, Warangesda, 240 kilometres north of Maloga, which another missionary, John Gribble, had founded in 1880.[5]

By 1884 Cooper had returned to Maloga, where he decided to follow the rest of his brothers and sisters in converting to Christianity. 'I must give my heart to God', he told Daniel Matthews after a service one day. In June that year he married a Yorta Yorta woman, Annie Clarendon Murrie. They were to have two children, only one of whom survived, before Annie died in 1889. By this time Cooper and other Yorta Yorta had moved onto Cumeroogunga, a supervised reserve or station founded nearby in 1886–87 by the New South Wales Aborigines Protection Board after Matthews had lost the confidence of his backers, the Aborigines Protection Association.[6] Cumeroogunga meant 'our home' in the Yorta Yorta language. There, in 1893, Cooper married Agnes Hamilton, a woman from Coranderrk, a Victorian reserve whose people had been closely associated with Maloga and Cumeroogunga. They had six children together before Agnes's death in 1910.[7]

Cumeroogunga flourished in its first twenty or so years, becoming the Protection Board's most successful station. Aboriginal people cleared 365 hectares of the 1200-hectare reserve and cultivated it in small family blocks. The income they derived from harvests of wheat and other crops was supplemented by the wages the men were able to command on pastoral properties in the district or further afield, while their families fished, cultivated vegetables and fruit, and raised cattle on the station. From 1908, however, the people's livelihood was increasingly threatened by a series of Board policies. Originally, their farming was frustrated by a lack of capital, later by the Board, which demanded they work the land for the Board's own coffers and withdrew the Aboriginal men's right to farm independently. The Board's seizure of the family blocks caused much bitterness and led to a series of confrontations between the people and the station manager. Many were expelled on disciplinary grounds. Cooper, it would seem, was among them (**97**); in the 1930s one of his associates related that Cooper 'had a quarrel with the Manager and moved to Victoria and had a little home near the Murray'.[8]

This must have been a severe blow to Cooper and his family, but he managed to earn a living throughout the 1910s and 1920s by working as a shearer, drover, horse-breaker and general rural labourer in Queensland, South Australia, New South Wales and Victoria. It was, not surprisingly, 'a very hard life'. During this period he was a member of the Australian Workers' Union and acted as a spokesman for Aboriginal workers in western New South Wales and central Victoria. He had, according to one of his political supporters in the 1930s, a 'longing to help his people'.[9]

In the early 1930s, Cooper, now in his seventies, returned to Cumeroogunga. This followed his third marriage, to Sarah Nelson née McCrae, another Coranderrk woman, in 1928. In 1933 they left the station, this time in order for Cooper to become eligible for an old age pension.[10] They settled in Melbourne, where they rented a series of houses in Footscray and Yarraville and became part of a small, impoverished community of a hundred or so Aboriginal people, most of whom congregated in Fitzroy and other inner-city suburbs after fleeing Cumeroogunga or reserves controlled by the Victorian Board for the Protection of Aborigines. Margaret Tucker, a member of the Australian Aborigines' League, later recalled meeting in one of the houses Cooper rented. It had neither gas nor electricity and they sat around the fire, 'the candles flickering on the mantelpiece'. Yet, by moving off a government station, Cooper won the freedom to take up his people's cause. For the next seven years of his life he devoted himself to this. He and his wife remained in Melbourne until 1940 when, his health failing, they decided to return to Cooper's own country. He died shortly afterwards, on 29 March 1941, and was buried at Cumeroogunga.[11]

In many respects Cooper was typical of Aboriginal political leaders in the 1920s and 1930s — and even the post-war years — in the most intensely colonised areas of Australia. Unlike the men who led protest at Coranderrk in the 1870s and 1880s, one of the first formally organised Aboriginal political campaigns in Australia,[12] Cooper's authority as a spokesman does not appear to have had a customary basis. Instead, it seems to have rested on the broad historical experience he had acquired as a result of living and working in the general community for many years. During much of his life Cooper enjoyed many of the legal rights and privileges of other Australians, largely escaping the most severe of the special laws that increasingly blighted the lives of Aboriginal people in settled areas. However, he knew of these and the suffering they caused, and he, too, had fallen foul of discriminatory laws in his later years. More generally, his life was determined by the lack of opportunities afforded

Aboriginal people; for example, he had little money and his formal education amounted only to several months of regular schooling as a child and some literacy classes as an adult.

Cooper's mission education nevertheless shaped much of his political work. (In recent decades Aboriginal and non-Aboriginal critics of missionary work have derided more than they have understood the work of missionaries and their impact on Aboriginal people.) Cooper's mentor, Daniel Matthews, represented a tradition of humanitarianism that influenced Aboriginal affairs from time to time throughout the nineteenth and twentieth centuries. Like an earlier generation of humanitarians in the 1830s and 1840s, Matthews believed indigenous people had 'valid claims on the Government' of the Australian colonies: the original landowners had been 'robbed…of their birthright' and had barely received any 'compensation'. More importantly, Matthews' evangelical work provided Cooper and other Yorta Yorta with powerful ways of understanding and protesting against their plight, and so helped equip them to fight for equality. First, Christian teachings were a powerful antidote to racism for Aborigines, as for other colonised peoples, since they proclaimed a vision of humanity that encompassed Aborigines, treating all peoples as God's children (**15, 63**). Second, they presented God and religious principles as a form of authority that was distinct from and higher than government and its secular principles, and so was another source to which Aborigines could appeal (**2, 4, 25, 63**). Third, Christianity offered a prophetic or predictive sense of history, a perspective on the unfolding of historical time that promised salvation for the downtrodden (**6, 40, 43, 56, 63**).[13]

More particularly, Matthews encouraged the Yorta Yorta to identify with the Jews of the Bible. He did so both through teachings, especially from the Old Testament, and his music, which included hymns and spirituals such as 'There is a happy land, Far, far away'.[14] In his old age, Cooper still recalled the Matthews' guidance and teachings (**97**), which had helped those gathered at Maloga to formulate a sense of themselves as a people, or, to use the language of the day, as a race. Most importantly, the historical narratives of the Bible, especially the Book of Exodus, encouraged them to envision themselves in terms akin to the persecuted and suffering Israelites (**40, 44, 53**). At the same time, this history offered them not just the hope but the unconditional promise of deliverance. According to God's binding covenant, the dispossessed who took their destiny into their own hands would eventually regain their place. Cooper and others at Maloga seem to have embraced this reassuring story of collective salvation. He once wrote: 'God's mercy endureth forever. Do right. Have faith in God...incline your heart anew unto the Lord...and the Lord will give thee victory over thine enemies'.[15]

As well as providing the Yorta Yorta with this religious framework, Matthews would also have introduced Cooper and others to the precepts of British liberal democracy, especially those regarding the rights and privileges of British citizens. Cooper undoubtedly embraced the ideal of British citizenship, believing, like indigenous leaders in other British colonies, that it was part and parcel of the highest form of democracy in the world. He often invoked British justice and fair play in his attacks on racial discrimination, while the Magna Carta, as the 'birthright' of all Englishmen, not surprisingly struck a chord with a leader whose people had been dispossessed of theirs (**25, 32, 37, 38, 50, 54, 62, 63, 72, 77, 82, 84, 93, 96**).

Much of Cooper's political work was provoked by the contemporary experience of his own people, as we shall see. However, there were ways in which it was also shaped by what had happened to his forebears and other Aborigines on the frontiers of settlement prior to his birth. In his appeals to government and public opinion Cooper recalled, time and time again, the violent treatment that Aboriginal people of his parents' and grandparents' generations had suffered (**8, 43, 46, 53, 63, 84**).

The petition

Soon after moving to Melbourne in 1933 Cooper took up the cause of his people by writing a letter to the editor of one of the city's newspapers (**8**). It was an approach already adopted by his brother-in-law, Thomas James, and James's son, Shadrach. Thomas James was a European-educated Tamil who had married one of Cooper's sisters, Ada Cooper. He had been the schoolteacher at Maloga and Cumeroogunga and was a greatly respected and much loved figure there. Since the late 1920s the James's had campaigned for Aboriginal rights in Melbourne, calling on the federal government to adopt a programme of reform (**3–7**). There were marked similarities between their proposals for change and those that Cooper soon began to advocate.

Among these proposals was a call for parliamentary representation for Aborigines. This was the central demand of Cooper's famous petition to King George V, which he launched in September 1933 (**10**). The petition was Cooper's most important cause, and his name and the organisation he founded were closely associated with it. One historian, Russell McGregor, has argued that the petition was 'overshadowed' in Cooper's political work 'by the grander issues of the uplift of the Aboriginal race and the granting of citizenship rights', but this obscures the fact that it continued to occupy a very important place in Cooper's mind and in his campaigning. He pressed the main claim of the petition repeatedly during the 1930s (**35, 50, 52–55, 58, 65, 69, 93, 96, 99**). As such, it warrants considerable attention.[16]

Petitioning government was an important political technique in Britain and her colonies during the nineteenth century. Indeed, Cooper had done this in the 1880s, when he and other Yorta Yorta men appealed to government for grants of land (**1, 2**). Petitioning government was less common in the twentieth century and petitioning the imperial monarch even less so. Nevertheless, Jane Duren, an elderly Aboriginal woman in New South Wales, had appealed to King George V in 1926 over the loss of reserve lands and other matters. The following year the Australian Aboriginal Progressive Association discussed it at a well-reported meeting in Sydney, and Cooper had probably heard of this. However, Cooper's idea of petitioning the King had deeper roots than this.[17]

There was a strongly held belief among Aboriginal people on New South Wales reserves, as well as on Coranderrk, that Queen Victoria had granted their reserve lands to them (**98**), just as there was a strong belief among indigenous people in New Zealand, South Africa and other British colonies in the Queen's bounty. As a result, historian Heather Goodall has pointed out, there was an assumption that their rights had been recognised 'at the highest levels of the British state'. Cooper, as a resident of Maloga and Cumeroogunga, to which many Coranderrk residents had fled between the 1870s and 1890s, probably shared this historical understanding. Thus, it is not surprising that he considered an appeal to one of Queen Victoria's successors.[18]

Fundamental to the tradition regarding Queen Victoria was a belief that Aborigines had a special relationship with the British monarch.

Given the important place of reciprocity in Aboriginal culture, it is probable that Cooper saw the King in terms of a kinship relationship. He often emphasised Aborigines' loyalty to King George V (**37, 71, 80**) and implied that the monarch had an obligation to honour. At the same time, Cooper believed that the King continued to have the right to intervene in Aboriginal matters, and maintained that Aborigines had a special right of appeal on the grounds that the Crown had reserved certain powers in respect of Aborigines (**50**). Other Aborigines who shared Cooper's historical experience and knowledge also recommended petitioning the King. In the same month that Cooper launched his petition a New South Wales Aboriginal spokesman, Joe Anderson, otherwise known as King Burraga, called a meeting to consider a petition to the King. He, too, called for representation in the federal parliament (**12**).[19]

Cooper's petitioning of the British monarch also probably owed something to his knowledge of and interest in Maori political representation. This might have derived from time he spent working in New Zealand, though he and Shadrach James had a strong interest in the status of other indigenous peoples and were familiar with government policies and practices concerning them (**7, 13, 63**). In the late nineteenth and early twentieth centuries Maori had petitioned Queen Victoria and her successor to the throne on several occasions and even travelled to England to present their appeals to her authority. Cooper frequently referred to the fact of Maori representation in the New Zealand parliament (**10, 21, 25, 39, 44, 51, 54, 63**) — four Maori seats were created in 1867 — when advocating the principal demand of his petition.[20]

Cooper also saw his petition to the King in strategic terms. Like white organisations such as the Association for the Protection of Native Races and white activists such as Mary Bennett, Cooper appreciated the value of appealing to British opinion. He corresponded with the London-based Anti-Slavery and Aborigines Protection Society, whose campaigning for Aboriginal rights he greatly admired (**41, 44, 57**).

The content of the petition, like its origins, is also a matter of interpretation. It contained three demands, but there can be little doubt that Aboriginal representation in the national parliament was the primary one as far as Cooper was concerned (**65**). This is evident in the earliest political activity associated with the petition; having launched it, he tried to form a deputation of Aboriginal leaders to present the plea to the federal government (**19**). This is also apparent, though, in statements Cooper made in the late 1930s (**65, 69, 93, 96**).

Aboriginal representation was important to Cooper and the League for two reasons. Government policy was determined without any consideration of Aboriginal opinion, and Aboriginal people greatly resented this. Consequently, Cooper envisaged a Member of Parliament speaking on Aborigines' behalf, acting as an advocate for their interests and a champion of their rights (**51, 69**). This Aboriginal voice was particularly important, Cooper claimed, because Aboriginal perspectives differed markedly to those of whites. It was a matter of what Cooper called 'thinking black'. This, he insisted, was not something whites could readily do (**30, 63, 77**).

The petition not only called for an Aboriginal representative in parliament but also for the right to propose an MP; hence, Cooper called for someone 'to be Chosen by My People'. There are other reasons, too, for regarding the petition as an assertion of Aboriginality. Cooper and his associates decided it should be signed by Aborigines only, and he saw it as a means of reaching out to other Aboriginal people. As far as he was concerned, it was the duty of every Aboriginal person to sign it (**14**).[21]

The petition was Aboriginal too in the sense that its principal demand was not simply a demand for the same rights as other Australians. Its call for Aboriginal representation constituted a demand for a special right, a right for Aborigines on the basis of their being the indigenous people of the country. This was certainly how other Aboriginal campaigners, such as Bill Ferguson, secretary of the Aborigines Progressive Association, characterised it when, in contrast to Cooper, he expressed a preference for a campaign for 'ordinary citizen rights'.[22]

It might also be suggested that an assertion of Aboriginal sovereignty is evident in Cooper's call for Aboriginal representation. This possibility might seem far-fetched were it not for the fact that on one occasion Cooper called for an Aboriginal state (**53**). Significantly, this occurred when he decided in 1937 to finally forward the petition to the King.[23] It is also the only time when Cooper, who was a fluent speaker, literally speaks in the historical record (**53**). Ten years earlier a petition had been presented to the federal parliament calling for a 'model Aboriginal state'. It attracted serious attention, and there can be little doubt Cooper knew of this petition since Shadrach James supported its call for an Aboriginal state (**3**).[24]

Consideration of the petition reveals some of the basic assumptions that informed Cooper's political campaigning. Cooper's belief that the King retained the right to intervene in Aboriginal affairs depended on a premise regarding a particular historical relationship between Aborigines and the Crown. Cooper held that the Crown still had a responsibility to Aborigines because of responsibilities it had undertaken to fulfil in the past. As the petition states, the original commission issued by the Crown to the founders of the British colonies in Australia had strictly charged them with the task of caring for the indigenes (**12**). Cooper also drew attention to a gubernatorial proclamation of 1836 that similarly set forth the duties of colonists towards Aborigines. Most importantly, Cooper believed that the British and their descendants had an obligation to Aboriginal people because they had stolen the country, enriched themselves at the expense of the original owners, and never compensated them for this. He repeatedly referred to this in demanding government introduce reforms to benefit his people (**8, 10, 18, 25, 32, 37, 77**).

Before creating the petition, Cooper met other Aborigines in Melbourne to discuss it (**14**), but it is clear that he was also assisted by a non-Aboriginal person experienced in drawing up legal documents. (One of his closest associates later claimed that the Catholic Archbishop of Melbourne, Daniel Mannix, was responsible for its wording.) Beginning in mid-1933, Cooper spent much time writing to Aborigines and missionaries about the petition, seeking the permission of governments to circulate it, and later sending petitions out for signatures. This was often frustrating, since some government authorities were slow to reply, directed Cooper to other state agencies, or refused permission (**13–15, 18**). Nevertheless, it seems nearly 2000 signatures had been obtained by early 1935, though Cooper hoped to get another 4000 (**23**).[25]

In this work Cooper was assisted by both James and Helen Baillie, a white woman. The latter was a member of two humanitarian organisations in Melbourne: the Aboriginal Fellowship Group and the Victorian Aboriginal Group. She was also connected with the Association for the Protection of Native Races and the Anti-Slavery Society, and advocates like the anthropologist A. P. Elkin and Mary

Bennett. Baillie knew other white people who could lend their support to Cooper's cause, such as the missionary and author Rev. Ernest Gribble in North Queensland and N. M. Morley, the secretary of the Australian Aborigines Amelioration Association in Western Australia, and she put Cooper in touch with these men. She probably also advised Cooper of the relevant government agencies and officials in Aboriginal affairs, and helped arrange interviews with federal government politicians and church leaders, such as the meeting in January 1935 (**25**). Baillie had considerable knowledge of Aboriginal matters elsewhere in Australia as a result of her own campaigning, and she would also have passed on information, newspaper articles, books and pamphlets to Cooper.[26]

By 1935 it seems that Cooper had become disheartened and was feeling the logistical and financial burdens of campaigning, the result of his limited education and income. Whereas he sent at least thirteen letters to government in 1933–34, he only wrote two in 1935 (or so the archival record indicates). In the early months of 1936, though, Cooper's cause received a considerable fillip. He met Arthur Burdeu, a white man who was to become an important ally. Like Cooper, Burdeu was a trade unionist, but more importantly he was also a devout Christian. He belonged to the Church of Christ, a church that gave each congregation considerable autonomy and which sponsored an Aboriginal pastor at Cumeroogunga. The two men lived quite close to one another but they used to confer in the city at Spencer Street railway station, where Burdeu worked, a long walk that Cooper made in order to save money to fight for his cause.[27]

Australian Aborigines' League

In 1936 the Australian Aborigines' League was established as a formally constituted body with a name, a platform and elected office-bearers. Before this, Cooper had made representations to government on behalf of a loose grouping of Aboriginal people, which he had variously called the Australian Aborigines' League, the Real Australian Aboriginal Society, and the Real Australian Native Society. The League's creation owed much to Arthur Burdeu.

According to the League's constitution, presumably drawn up by Burdeu, full membership was open only to Aborigines, while 'administrative positions' were to be 'primarily' filled by them (**31**). The principle of Aboriginal control was reflected in the organisation's name, the Australian Aborigines' League. The possessive apostrophe was important. Cooper, who became the League's secretary, and his Aboriginal associates saw it as *their* organisation and regarded themselves as *the* spokespersons for Aboriginal people (**10, 23, 25, 37**). As Cooper stated soon after the League was formed, this was 'the Dark Man's own ameliorative effort for his own race'. The League's first annual report made the point more bluntly: 'This is Our Movement.'[28]

The League was not only an Aboriginal organisation at the outset; it continued to be one. This partly can be attributed to Cooper's forceful personality. He had, Burdeu remarked in 1940, 'very definite opinions' and impressed them upon associates like Burdeu and Baillie. However, Burdeu also played an important role in this. Although he became president of the League soon after its formation and helped formulate its objectives, he worked in a manner sympathetic to the Aboriginal members' aspirations. He strongly believed Aborigines should be in the forefront of the political struggle for Aboriginal rights and that this would advance the cause considerably. Burdeu also recognised that the League was a distinctive organisation because, in his words, it represented 'the aboriginal problem from the dark man's point of view'. 'The League,' he asserted, was 'the Aboriginal Voice'. Most importantly, Burdeu respected Cooper's leadership of the League and tried hard to help Cooper and other members articulate their own objectives. He realised they were not 'properly vocal' and patiently assisted them 'to express their needs'.[29]

Following the formation of the League, Cooper authorised and signed letters from it as its secretary but he wrote very few of these. As Cooper himself observed, his lack of education meant he found letter-writing a difficult task. The differences in handwriting, grammar, spelling and punctuation between the letters he wrote and those drawn up by others are obvious (compare, for example, **14** and **36**). However, there are no grounds for believing that the letters that appeared over Cooper's name do not basically represent his point of view, just as there is no evidence that Cooper ever objected to the form and content of any letters prepared in his name. Instead, there seems to have been a harmonious meeting of minds. In writing letters in Cooper's name it seems that Burdeu and others worked closely with Cooper, listening to what he said and trying to capture the essence of his ideals, goals and demands. Consequently, there is much consistency in the content of the letters, just as there are marked similarities between these and the interview Cooper gave the journalist Clive Turnbull in 1937 (**53**). For these reasons we have concluded that these letters *do* represent Cooper's views. This said, there can be no doubt that Burdeu tempered Cooper's anger in most of his pleas to government. In 1940 he observed that he had 'tried to keep [Cooper] from any drastic step', just as Baillie divulged that she had sought earlier to persuade him 'that constructive work [was] better than destructive'.[30]

Many of the letters, it can also be argued, have a distinctively personal mode of address. This is common among a people for whom speaking and listening remains a more important form of communication than reading and writing, and where kinship continues to be the dominant cultural code shaping relationships between people. In many of his letters to government Cooper addresses ministers as though he were speaking directly to family or friends (for example, **44, 47, 51**).[31]

The League's programme

In 1936 William Cooper, Arthur Burdeu and other members formulated a programme for the Australian Aborigines' League. Unlike Cooper's petition, the main focus of this was on gaining civil rights rather than indigenous rights. The solution to the problems Aboriginal people faced, they held, lay in reversing racial discrimination in all its forms, particularly the denial of civil rights, and in reforms that gave Aborigines the opportunity for advancement. Consequently, the League's approach was non-racial for the most part. It was demanding the same rights other Australians enjoyed, as well as inclusion in the Australian community. In campaigning for these demands, furthermore, Cooper and the League emphasised that Aborigines were fellow human beings and had the capacity for 'uplift', and explicitly rejected the racism that denied them their humanity or treated them as inferior beings (**30, 31, 33, 37–39, 42, 51, 57, 63, 64, 66, 70, 73, 91, 96, 99**).

The League's call for civil rights and uplift was informed by an influential theory of historical progress that held that the course of history involved a natural progression through four stages. Human societies began with primitive hunter-gathering and developed through pastoralism and agriculture to 'modern' commerce and industry. Like missionary and humanitarian organisations and campaigners in the inter-war period, the Australian Aborigines' League distinguished between three stages or groups of Aborigines — primitive, semi-civilised and detribalised, and civilised — and advocated different policies for each. They foresaw a future in which Aboriginal people would advance through these stages and eventually become fully civilised or modern. They called for citizenship for the last group only, since they, like other campaigners, believed that Aborigines needed to be civilised before they assumed all the rights and privileges of a citizen (**5, 6, 25, 31, 34, 38, 42, 44, 45, 51, 62, 78, 96**).[32]

Yet, while Cooper and the League wholeheartedly embraced equal rights and advocated the inclusion of Aborigines in modern Australia, they often made their demands for this by reference to 'racial difference'. In calling for opportunities for Aboriginal 'uplift', which in itself could be regarded as a demand for special rights for a disadvantaged people, they repeatedly made claims in which they referred to their ancestors' ownership of the land and their dispossession. Prior Aboriginal ownership of the land did not necessarily constitute the *basis* of the League's claims, however. Aboriginal spokespersons undoubtedly invoked their indigeneity in the course of making demands for rights but they usually drew back from demanding the rights of indigenous peoples. Instead, they asserted their indigeneity so they could make a stronger claim for the civil rights that other Australians enjoyed. Who had a greater right to such privileges than the original inhabitants? they asked (**1, 4, 6, 7, 30, 37, 38, 50, 53, 62, 63, 69, 77, 98, 100**). In doing this they often compared their lack of rights to the rights that 'aliens' such as the Chinese had been granted (**39, 48, 66, 77, 78, 93, 95, 96**).

Cooper and the League none the less questioned the dominant racial order. First, by demanding the same rights that white Australians enjoyed, they challenged its premises. To claim a common nature with whites was to deny whites' assumption of superiority. In calling for 'A fair deal for the dark race' — this was the League's motto — Cooper's organisation was demanding for 'dark' Aborigines what had been reserved exclusively for 'fair' whites. Cooper, moreover, challenged the categories of whiteness, Australianness and Britishness when he demanded for Aborigines the right to be British, and asserted that Aborigines deserved a place alongside their fellow Australians (**44, 45, 50, 61, 69, 92**).

Second, the League's spokespersons challenged white Australia not so much by deploying their indigeneity — that is, their status as the descendants of the original peoples — but by invoking their Aboriginality in the sense of being a distinctive group or race of people. Cooper, for example, commonly spoke of Aborigines as 'a people' (see, for example, **50**), and one of the most significant features of the League's policy was its rejection of absorption as well as the assumption, which often informed this policy, that a distinction could be made between 'full blood' and 'half-caste' Aborigines (**37, 38, 42, 50, 51, 77, 86**). At the same time that Cooper and the League criticised this policy, and asserted their vision of Aboriginal people as a permanent or ongoing community in Australia, they also rejected white control. Indeed, the importance they placed on Aborigines playing a role in governing themselves was one of the most persistent strands in their campaigning (**5, 7, 25, 36, 42, 48, 54, 68, 71, 72, 82**).

Cooper's sense of 'race' rested on foundations that were very different to the ones that underpinned European racial science and popular racism. It was rooted in a historical conception of Aborigines as an indigenous people who had suffered and continued to suffer the effects of colonisation (**29, 38, 40, 43, 44, 50, 53, 63, 92, 97**). In this respect it is apparent that Cooper and other members of the League saw themselves as a racial minority and identified very strongly with other such peoples (**44, 50, 71, 72, 87, 92, 96, 99, 100**). The historical suffering that Cooper and other members of the League focused on most often was not their people's original dispossession, even though they often referred to the killings committed by white frontiersmen (**4, 7, 8, 53, 57**). Rather, it was the later losses they suffered, especially those experienced at Cumeroogunga, which, we have noted, began in the first decade of the twentieth century. Most of the office-bearers and executive members of the League had been expelled, removed or forced from the station but they continued to regard it as their home.[33] Despite their displacement, or perhaps because of it, they continued to have a strong sense of community and identity that was rooted in their own historical experiences as well as those of the Kulin, Pangerang and Yorta Yorta who had been forced off Coranderrk in the 1870s and 1880s.

As far as those like Cooper were concerned, these people had demanded and won land in the 1880s (**1**), farmed it well in the 1890s and 1900s, only to lose this security, have their independence undermined, and find their families and community broken up and forced from their homeland by a repressive Board in the 1910s and 1920s. These experiences were woven into a collective memory of loss, oppression and expulsion. This history was often told over the following years by people such as Shadrach James and Anna Morgan (**6, 24**), as well as by Cooper (**25**), and it clearly shaped much of the League's policy.[34]

A considerable part of the League's campaigning focused on the need for land, capital and other resources for Aboriginal people. Indeed, it regarded education (**24, 31, 33, 39, 42, 45, 50, 51, 53, 57, 62, 64, 73, 75, 84, 90, 95, 99**) and the security and development of reserve and other lands as the keys to Aboriginal advancement (**1, 31, 36, 39, 41, 42, 62, 99**). In particular, Cooper argued that Cumeroogunga should be developed as a model station, an example of what could be achieved by Aborigines who were provided with proper government support (**39, 48**). Likewise, the League protested vigorously against the deteriorating social and economic conditions on stations, particularly Cumeroogunga (**30, 47, 48, 59**). Yet, Cooper was also 'a great advocate for getting out and working instead of hanging about the Mission' (by which he meant supervised reserves), and of converting reserves into small farms for Aborigines (**37**).[35]

A good deal of the League's work was intensely local, just as earlier Aboriginal protest had been. Cooper and the League, though, were determined to develop policies that addressed the needs of Aboriginal people throughout Australia, as the organisation's constitution demonstrates (**31**). Cooper saw himself as campaigning on behalf of all Aborigines, whom he called his countrymen and his native people (**14, 32, 53**), and the League presented itself as a national organisation representing all Aborigines. Such representation was very difficult to achieve, but the League did actively campaign for Aboriginal rights in several states, including Western Australia (**64, 67, 68, 72, 79**), and it frequently called for federal control of Aboriginal affairs (**25, 36, 37, 42, 57, 63, 93, 94**). Its broad vision owed much to Cooper's knowledge of other parts of Australia.

In its protest the League employed the moderate political methods sanctioned by the Australian political system. It held public meetings and concerts, sent letters to the editors of newspapers, and, most of all, addressed appeals to government (see, for example, **49**). It eschewed what Cooper called 'the methods of agitators' and sought to make constructive appeals to government (**40, 61, 84**). In their work Cooper and the other League leaders seem to have assumed that injustice prevailed because white Australians did not know the facts of what had happened and was happening to Aboriginal people. As a result they saw their task as one of enlightening the Australian public about the true situation of Aborigines, creating a body of public opinion sympathetic to their plight and thus putting pressure on governments to adopt new policies (**28, 50, 58, 61, 63, 84, 87, 90**).

The League, as we have seen, was regarded by its members as an Aboriginal organisation and they were committed to articulating Aboriginal perspectives. However, it was by no means separatist in its approach to campaigning. It tried to cultivate good relationships with white bodies sympathetic to its cause, and to work with and alongside white organisations devoted to Aboriginal reform. Its closest relationships were with humanitarian organisations that were similarly pro-missionary, such as the Association for the Protection of Native Races in Sydney, the Australian Aborigines Amelioration Association in Perth and the Anti-Slavery and Aborigines Protection Society in London (**29, 32, 35, 38, 41, 45, 52, 57, 71**). In the late 1930s, though, the League also forged close relationships with the left, including communists, particularly in the context of the walk-off from Cumeroogunga, which will be discussed shortly (**67, 68, 72, 90**).

Some advocates for Aboriginal rights were critical of the League. These detractors included humanitarian campaigners. Amy Brown, the secretary of the Victorian Aboriginal Group, reckoned Burdeu was the League's 'President, Secretary & Committee'. The anthropologist Donald Thomson regarded only so-called traditional Aborigines as Aborigines, and consequently cast doubt on the Aboriginality of the League's leaders, claiming the League's petition to King George VI owed 'its driving force to others than aborigines'. Other activists similarly romanticised 'traditional Aborigines', for example the trade unionist and Communist Party member Tom Wright, who was highly critical of 'the policy of the so-called "Australian Aborigines League"' since he was convinced people of 'mixed blood' should be absorbed into the white community. The League, in turn, complained bitterly about the racial representations of anthropologists and their acolytes who focused solely on the needs of indigenous people in northern and central Australia and advocated a policy of segregation (**44, 57, 63**).[36]

The League found it easier to work with Aboriginal rather than non-Aboriginal organisations so long as these were not dominated by white advocates like the conservative ultra-nationalist P. R. Stephensen (who advised Jack Patten and the Aborigines Progressive Association in New South Wales). Yet, the League also came into conflict with Aboriginal critics like the conservative South Australian spokesman David Unaipon, who regarded its proposal for the now famous Day of Mourning as too political (**61**).[37]

The Day of Mourning

At times William Cooper and his fellow Aboriginal leaders seem to have believed that both government and the public were taking a keener interest in their cause (**37, 52**), but these bouts of optimism alternated with periods of pessimism, even despair (**40, 50, 51, 54, 63**). Cooper was often forced to acknowledge that governments, at least in the states, did not take the League seriously, since they questioned the standing of organisations that only comprised 'natives'.[38]

In the autumn of 1937 Cooper seemed confident that both state and federal governments would introduce some of the reforms he had been urging but his hopes were dashed over the next few months. This provoked him to send a series of letters to the Premier of New South Wales, Bertram Stevens (see, for example, **66**). More importantly, Cooper decided the time had come to send his petition to the King, now George VI. Cooper, or more especially his white advisers, had seen the petition as a bargaining tool that would only be used when other avenues of appeal had been exhausted (**50**), which is why it had not been presented earlier.

The first-ever national conference of administrators of Aboriginal affairs in April 1937 had humiliated Aborigines, Cooper complained in June (**50**). He promised to withhold the petition a little longer. By August, though, he had had enough (**53**) and Burdeu forwarded the petition to the government on his behalf.[39] A month or so passed.

An acknowledgment was finally sent, not in the name of Prime Minister Joseph Lyons but that of his secretary. This promised that consideration would be given to the petition but made reference to the Commonwealth's limited jurisdiction in Aboriginal affairs, and it claimed the Commonwealth and state governments were doing everything they could to address Aboriginal problems. Cooper was enraged (**54**). In October he and the League decided to publicise the petition (**55**), and in November he and Burdeu called a meeting to decide further action, where it was agreed to hold a 'Day of Mourning' (**56**).

The Day of Mourning was not Cooper's idea alone — the other key mover was Bill Ferguson — but there can be no doubt about his part in it. The proposal was very similar to one Cooper made at this time for an 'Aborigines' Day', to be held every year on the Sunday closest to Australia Day (**61**).[40] (This was soon instituted by churches and came to be known as 'Aboriginal Sunday'.) More significantly, the proposed day of mourning undoubtedly reflected Cooper's historical sensibility. As discussed earlier, many mission-educated Aborigines like Cooper had a predictive or prophetic view of history. They imagined a relationship between the past, present and future as a long trajectory marked by epochs and days — of 'Judgment' and 'Restitution', 'Mourning' and 'Hope' — at the end of which there would surely be deliverance for their people from the suffering that was their lot, just as there was for the Jews (**6, 43, 63**). This religious perspective provided an alternative view of how historical time (or 'the course of history') could unfold, challenging the settler account of Australian history as the triumph of white progress.

Cooper's idea for a day of mourning probably also arose out of a particular experience of this settler Australian history he and his fellow members of the League had had in January 1937. They had attended a 'Grand Pioneer Rally and Historical Service' to celebrate John Batman's founding of Melbourne and, more generally, the anniversary of Australia. This event, attended by some 2000 people, had been orchestrated by Isaac Selby, the septuagenarian secretary of an organisation of colonists, the Old Pioneers' Memorial Fund. The League members led the singing that began the afternoon's programme, which included 'Rule Britannia' and 'God Save the King', and they played the part of 'the aborigines' in a pageant at the close of the commemoration that represented Batman's discovery of the

Yarra River in Melbourne. Cooper and his people went with some misgivings but the day turned out worse than they expected as a result of several speeches that formed the centre of the afternoon's programme. They were not so much troubled by Selby's speech. While he spoke of Batman as 'an Empire Builder' it is likely that he also referred to Batman's treaty with the Kulin, which was regarded highly by Cooper and other Aboriginal people since they interpreted it as recognition of their status as the original landowners (**33, 43, 78, 81**).[41] Instead, it was a speech given by Mr G. R. Holland, the chief president of the Australian Natives Association, that dismayed Cooper. (The ANA had championed the cause of white Australian 'natives' since the 1870s and had sought to appropriate the status of 'indigenous' for white Australians.) Holland's peroration, entitled 'Our Island Continent', provoked Cooper to write to Selby a few days later (**43**).[42]

In this letter, Cooper's conviction that Aboriginal people should commemorate the beginning of European colonisation in a distinctive manner is explicit. In fact, Aboriginal people like Cooper had long believed that white celebrations of their settlement of the continent should be an occasion for reflecting on the dispossession of Aborigines and ways of addressing this (**1**). Selby, who made his living by giving public lectures and putting on lantern shows and pageants on historical subjects, responded to Cooper's angry letter by inviting Cooper and the League to participate in a concert to celebrate Melbourne's 102nd birthday in May. This was eventually held in the Australian Church in Russell Street, Melbourne, thus anticipating the Day of Mourning, which was held in the Australian Hall in Elizabeth Street, Sydney, the following January (**49**).[43]

Just as Cooper's suspicion that the federal government was going to ignore his petition contributed to his proposal of a day of mourning, its unambiguous rejection of the petition in February 1938 led him to formulate a long political statement, which he sent to Lyons the following month.[44] Entitled 'From an Educated Black', it can be regarded as Cooper's political testament (**63**). It resembles the forthright statements Shadrach James had made several years earlier, and James probably had a hand in writing it.[45]

The mounting frustration Cooper felt at this time is evident in other ways. On several occasions between 1938 and 1940 he made comparisons between the treatment of his people and the persecution of Jews and other minorities in Nazi Germany (**68, 72, 78, 84, 99, 100**), and in December 1938 the League formed a delegation to the German consulate in Melbourne to protest against this (**76**).[46] Yet, it was the deteriorating conditions of life on his beloved homeland of Cumeroogunga that most provoked Cooper's anger at this time, prompting some of his most strongly worded attacks on government.

Cumeroogunga walk-off

During the 1920s and 1930s, conditions on New South Wales stations worsened considerably. The Aborigines Protection Board had pushed many Aboriginal people off supervised reserves and allowed these to run down, only to reverse its policy when economic depression led to massive unemployment and white town dwellers complained about the presence of Aborigines in townships, calling for their removal. As a result, the number of Aboriginal people on stations increased from 6788 in 1927 to 10 467 in 1937, and the living conditions deteriorated further. As we have noted, Cooper had been protesting about these for some time but he complained more vehemently now (**59, 74**), as did Jack Patten, president of the Aborigines Progressive Association (**75**).

Most of all, many of the residents of Cumeroogunga, and Cooper and the League in turn, sorely resented the way Aboriginal people there were treated by the manager and matron who had been appointed to take over the station in mid-1937 (**71**). The previous manager, J. G. Danvers, who understood the people's grievances regarding the loss of land there, supported its development and was respected by the residents (**47**), was transferred to another station. He was replaced by Arthur McQuiggan, who was moved rather than dismissed from his position as superintendent of Kinchela Aboriginal Boys' Home after repeated complaints about the brutal beatings he administered to his young charges.[47] McQuiggan and his wife were harsh and authoritarian, and conflict broke out soon after they assumed control of Cumeroogunga.

The residents complained to both Cooper and Patten, and drew up a petition to the Board seeking the McQuiggans' removal. Cooper went to Cumeroogunga to investigate and then protested vigorously to the Board (**74**). It sent the petition back to Cumeroogunga, where McQuiggan tried to intimidate those who had signed. This further enraged residents, Cooper and the League (**84**). The crisis deepened when the residents heard reports suggesting that new regulations were to be introduced which would confine them to the stations. Most troubling of all, though, was a rumour that children were to be removed. This awakened the community's worst fears. Children had been forcibly taken from stations in this area on a number of occasions between 1915 and 1919, including Margaret Tucker, an executive member of the League (**85**). William Morley, the secretary of the Association for the Protection of Native Races, observed that the removals from Cumeroogunga in 1919 had remained 'in the[ir] memory' such that there was 'a reasonable fear that "It [was] 1919 [all] over again"'. McQuiggan's habit of moving around the station with a rifle aggravated other fears, ones which remained strong in what Cooper once called Aborigines' 'racial memory' (**53, 84**).[48]

In February 1939 Patten and his brother, George, visited Cumeroogunga and persuaded many of the residents they should 'strike'. They crossed the Murray River in boats and camped on the riverbank near the township of Barmah, where a number of their kin had been living since the early 1920s. It is difficult to know how many people left, as the reports of the walk-off gave wildly conflicting estimates. Most likely, a hundred or so men, women and children abandoned their homes.[49]

The League largely became responsible for taking up the cause of the people at Cumeroogunga (**83, 84, 87–89**) and supporting them. It received considerable support from left-wing unionists and Communist Party members in Melbourne, who eventually formed a new organisation, the Aborigines Assistance Committee. George Patten became its organiser, and Eric Onus and Margaret Tucker represented the League on it (**90**). (Cooper was ill during much of this period.) However, the League lacked the resources to sustain the walk-off and many of the residents were forced to either return to the station or move away altogether. Some recalled the walk-off as a defiant blow for freedom, others as a bitter and costly defeat.[50]

By the time the walk-off was over, Australia was embroiled in another European war. In March 1938 Burdeu, on behalf of the League, had suggested that an 'Aboriginal citizen corps' be formed, a proposal which implied that military service should result in Aborigines being granted citizenship. Interest in the formation of an identifiably Aboriginal force grew among other Aboriginal organisations. In December Jack Patten, representing the Aborigines Progressive Association, put forward a plan similar to the League's. The following month, however, a disenchanted Cooper, who had lost one of his sons in World War I, angrily informed the Minister for the Interior, John McEwen, that his organisation's support for an Aboriginal unit was now conditional. The past and present actions of Australian governments had made them unworthy of the loyalty of Aborigines, who had fought in the last war only to return home to the inferior status they had long had. Furthermore, they had no country to fight for since they had been dispossessed of all their land. Until all racial discrimination was removed, there should be no Aboriginal enlistment, let alone the establishment of Aboriginal regiments (**80**).[51]

The beginning of the war in September 1939 gave the League and other organisations an opportunity to press the demand for citizenship. In October and December 1939, and again in August 1940, Cooper argued that the war had broken out because of Hitler's discriminatory treatment of minorities and that consequently Australia could not honestly fight fascism while it was still oppressing its Aboriginal minority. This could only be rectified by the government granting citizenship rights to civilised Aborigines (**92, 96, 99**). The Australian armed services, however, came to believe that the enlistment of people of non-European origin was neither desirable nor necessary, and so were reluctant to admit Aborigines (though many did in fact volunteer and were accepted).[52] In March 1941, a couple of days after Cooper died, Burdeu claimed that the army had discharged Aboriginal men who had joined up, many of whose loyalty had been severely weakened as a result. Some had remarked, he told the Prime Minister's office, 'We have no King now and no country.' A few months later another campaigner, Bill Onus, told Prime Minister John Curtin that the Commonwealth's failure to grant citizenship, particularly to Aboriginal servicemen, had weakened his people's support for the war effort. Some resented their discriminatory treatment so much that they had become quite indifferent, 'their attitude being summed up by one Native who [had] remarked that "the natives are being asked to fight to make Australia safe for those who took it from their people"'.[53]

A few years later Onus would join with Doug Nicholls in reviving Cooper's League, renewing his calls for both indigenous rights and citizenship rights and so sustaining his legacy during the post-war years. Nicholls recalled in the 1960s: 'Everything comes back to William Cooper … he fired me to follow through'. When a black power movement emerged in the late 1960s, Cooper's emphasis on 'thinking black' was championed by both elderly and young campaigners. A Victorian Tribal Council was founded along the same lines as the League, and soon after its formation Onus's brother Eric paid tribute to Cooper as the founder of an organisation 'which opened the way for us to carry on'. More recently, Cooper's work has helped inspire another generation of the Yorta Yorta to press a native title claim. 'One can be assured', one of their leaders has written, 'that Uncle William's words will continue to be the driving force of the Yorta Yorta struggle'.[54]

Documents

1. Maloga petition, 20 July 1887

To His Excellency the Right Hon. Baron Carrington, P.C., K.C.M.G. — Your Excellency. — The following of the Aborigines and half-castes on the Maloga Aboriginal Mission Station, and the neighborhood thereof, hereby showeth that while grateful for the benefits conferred upon them by the liberality of our Government, in aiding the Aborigines Protection Association to provide a home for them and their families, and also recognising their debt of gratitude to that association, they would suggest that on the recommendation of that society those among us, who so desires, should be granted sections of land of not less than 100 acres per family in fee simple or else at a small nominal rental annually, with the option of purchase at such prices as shall be deemed reasonable for them under the circumstances, always bearing in mind that the Aborigines were the former occupiers of the land. Such a provision would enable them to earn their own livelihood, and thus partially relieve the State from the burden of their maintenance. We think that such a provision would be far more in accord with the wishes of Her Most Gracious Majesty Queen Victoria in this the jubilee year of her reign than many of the methods adopted to celebrate that occasion, and also that it would be a fitting memorial in connection with the celebration of the Centenary of the colony. Trusting that your Excellency will see fit to grant our petition, your petitioners will, as in duty bound, ever pray. On behalf of the petitioners. — Robert Cooper, Samson Barber, Aaron Atkinson, Hughy Anderson, John Cooper, Edgar Atkinson, Whyman McLean, John Atkinson (his mark), William Cooper, George Middleton, Edward Joachim (his mark).

2. William Cooper to J. M. Chanter, MLA, 11 November 1887

I most respectfully beg to state that I shall feel deeply obliged if you will be good enough to use your influence toward securing a piece of land for me. I am anxious to get a home and make some provisions for my wife and daughter & as I am an Honest hard-working man, the land will be applied to a legitimate use. I want a grant of land that I can call my own so long as I and my family live and yet without the power of being able to do away with the land.

[With] Farming barely sufficient to maintain my family decently I find it therefore impossible to pay for a selection. I shall be perfectly satisfied with 100 acres adjoining the Maloga Aboriginal Reserve if possible. I do trust you will be successful in securing this small portion of a vast territory which is ours by Divine right. We know that grants of land have been made to aborigines in other parts of N.S.W. and that they have been abused but as there have been no grants made to our tribe I beg you to give us a trial. Hoping to get a favourable reply.
I have the honor to be
Sir
Your most obedient servant

3. *Sun* (Melbourne), 22 February 1929

"The proposal for establishing a native state is a commendable scheme, but I fear it is an impossibility with the present generation", writes Shadrach L. James, who describes himself as an aboriginal native of Barmah in a letter to the Minister for Home Affairs.

Commenting on the recent report on aborigines, Mr James suggests a start could be made for the ultimate realisation of the scheme, by educating and training natives for filling responsible positions in such a state.

Mr Abbott has expressed a wish to see Mr James at a conference in Melbourne shortly to discuss the welfare of aborigines.

4. *Sun* (Melbourne), 12 April 1929, S. L. James, address to the Australian National Missionary Council

"I can only express myself in crude and unpolished phrases," said Shadrach James.

"This massacre of my people has been going on for years and years.

"What have the whites done to help us in the past 80 years? There has never been a vigorous or decisive effort made to help us. Whatever efforts have been made to help us have been by the missionaries. They are the only people who have attempted to lift us to citizenship.

"What do you propose to do with us in the future? Do you propose to keep us in a servile state until we disappear as a people? If you believe in the God you have taught us, as I know you do, you will help us.

"Some people say the blacks have no intelligence, and are incapable of keeping any religious impression. I have seen many of my own people live and die in the faith.

"In the history of my people I only know of one instance where a person who has killed some of us has been punished.

Food Not Everything

"I do not believe in police protection for my people. What have the police done to help, uplift or teach us? They consider that rations and clothes are sufficient return for the inestimable benefits that white civilisation is gaining from the land we have lost."

5. *Herald* (Melbourne), 12 April 1929, 'Aborigine Wants M.P. for Natives'

"My People Seek Part in Country's Development"

Mr Shadrach Livingston James, a full-blooded aborigine, attended the conference today called by the Minister for Home Affairs (Mr Abbott) to discuss the Bleakley report on native problems. Mr James represented the aborigines.

Mr S. L. James is a full-blooded aborigine with the poise and cultured speech of the educated white man. Though still quite a young man, he is profound in his reflections on the problem of emancipating his people. He wants them to take their share in the development of the country of which he feels they are the rightful heirs.

His father was for some years a teacher in the Cummergunja district in N.S.W., but has now retired and is living in Melbourne. Mr James, senr., is noticeably proud of his clever son, and hopes to see him accomplish great things for the cause to which they are both whole-heartedly devoted.

Missionaries Praised

"The missionaries are the best help our people have", said Mr S. L. James today. "It is to their efforts that we owe what opportunities we have to raise the standard of our civilisation, and take our place in the modern world.

"Many of us are as intelligent and as well educated as lots of white men, but we cannot get the chance to prove our ability. Even Government departments discriminate against us.

"What we want is an aboriginal representative in Parliament, and a native administrator working for us under the direction of the Minister.

"The hearts of many of my people are burning with ambition, but the only way they can rise is with the aid and encouragement of the Government.

Civil Reforms Wanted

"Our lands have been taken, and for lack of opportunity we are a backward people. The missionaries have tried to teach as many of us as possible. Now we ask for proper scope to develop.

"I think that the spiritual leadership of the churches is of the greatest value, but it should be supplemented by reforms in the civil administration."

6. *Australian Intercollegian*, 1 May 1929, Shadrach James, 'The Wrongs of the Australian Aboriginal'

It is a tragic fact that the condition of my people still remains a problem for which all the wise heads of the Governments of this land, for a hundred years, have failed to find a satisfactory solution. The hearts of those of us who have been watching the trend of events in the history of our people, have been gladdened, from time to time, when there have come, from the voice and pen of some benevolent statesman, intimations of laudable schemes for our betterment, buoying us with the hope of a better day — which never came. So far there has never been a vigorous, resolute, decisive, and intensive effort to lift us up socially, intellectually, morally, and spiritually. Whenever and wherever such an effort has been put forth, we credit the missionaries for the experiment, and my people have responded well.

The Governments of Australia have had the Aborigines for over a century in their hands and have not yet taken them out of the experimental stage. What have they done to educate them to take their places worthily in the community? The Australian whites, with justifiable joy and pride, boast of their marvellous achievements in countless phases of life amongst their own people. What have they done and what are they doing for the uplift of my people? Do they consider the weekly ration, the annual supply of blankets and clothing, an adequate compensation for the inestimable benefits they are daily deriving from this land which, by divine right, belongs to us? The white man's answer to this is that the civilisation he has introduced has brought to us many compensating advantages. We grant that, and also gratefully acknowledge the debt we owe to the whites for the knowledge of the true God and His worship. But, alas! they have brought also vice, disease, and the curse of liquor. When will the Australians wake up to their national duty, their responsibility and obligation to us? They complain of our ingratitude. We ask, when will they pay the debt of gratitude they owe to us for the untold gain that has come to them through our irremediable loss?

To quote the words of one of your statesmen, Dr Basedow, *The Aborigine has not had a dog's chance*.[55] We wonder if we will ever, under present conditions, get a chance to lift up our heads. Although much dispirited, we have not lost heart. We still possess a residue of courage, ambition, and determination to strike out and secure a worthy place in the community if our protectors would, in the name of justice and humanity, give us an opportunity.

I would now draw your attention to some of the disabilities under which we suffer, and under the present administration there is no prospect of their being removed. There is a great deal of unemployment amongst my people, which accounts for their poverty and distress. With the exception of shearing and harvesting seasons, which absorb five months, we are practically out of employment for the rest of the year. During these months we do some fishing and trapping, which yield but a precarious living, and the consequence is nearly seventy-five per cent are living in a semi-starved condtion.

I venture to say without the least fear of refutation that twenty-five per cent of our men are quite capable of entering many fields of labour and, standing alongside of the white Australians, work equally as hard and as well as they. We have splendid axemen who could undertake sleeper hewing, forest thinning, road making, etc., but they are denied their licences and employment in these fields. Some of us are intellectually fit to fill some positions in the Government service — railways, tramways, forest and postal departments, etc., but we are debarred from taking these positions.

Reserves for the use of the Aborigines have been set apart in many places throughout the Commonwealth, and they are vested in the Aborigines' Protection Board, but the Aborigines are denied the right of using the land, and in some cases these reserves are leased to white men. Many of the reserves have river frontages, and could be cut up into irrigation blocks and allotted to the capable Aborigines, where they could settle permanently and make homes of their own without the fear of being disturbed.

I know of several Aborigines who were granted some 30 to 40 acres of land some years ago and were promised larger grants if they proved their capability of clearing and working this land. These men worked hard, their wives helping, on scanty supplies of ration, and fenced and cleared about 900 acres of densely timbered land, and just when they were expecting fair returns from their land the blocks were taken away from them, with no prospect of compensation for their labour.

Our girls, at the age of 14 years, are forcibly taken from their homes and sent out to service. We do not object to their being trained to work as domestic servants, but we strongly object to their being sent at that age when they need a mother's protection.

I wish to correct the general belief that our days are numbered. I say most emphatically that my people are not doomed to extinction. They may yet be saved. Let the authorities secure the needed legislation for their protection, betterment and preservation, and undertake the work of caring for them, not as heretofore, with the conviction they are a dying race, but with the confidence that the remnant can be saved. Here I wish to offer some constructive ideas and make some practical suggestions with reference to the care of my people.

I strongly advise the placing of all native aboriginals throughout the Commonwealth under the Federal Government. At present the care of the Aborigines is entrusted to an institution known as the Aborigines' Protection Board, which works through the Police Department. This Board, we understand, is a trustee to disburse to the best advantage the money appropriated by the State for our maintenance, education and general welfare. There are other responsibilities devolving upon the Board besides feeding clothing, and educating us. By the term Protection Board, we understand an institution which stands for promoting, encouraging, and, if need be, creating such influences that will make for our moral, social, intellectual development, and for intercepting those that are inimical to our advancement. In these things we must say the Board has not lived up to its responsibility. We have not made any real progress under their administration.

We desire the appointment of a Native Administrator, because he would be in sympathy with us and grasp more readily our needs, and for the same reason we ask for a native representative in the House, to voice our needs and disabilities, and a Native Protector in each State to see that our people were well cared for.

For the moral and spiritual care of my people, I advise the appointment of itinerant white and Aboriginal evangelists who shall visit the Aboriginals who are not connected with mission stations.

I am quite sure we are in the dawn of a new day for our people. I feel that the influences and prejudices that have been operating against us for a century, keeping us in a servile condition and withholding from us our natural rights, is now giving place to genuine sympathy for my people and a willingness on the part of our rulers to yield some substantial good to them.

7. *Herald* (Melbourne), 24 March 1930, Shadrach James, 'Help my People! Native Preacher's Strong Plea: Case for the Aborigines'

It is gratifying to note that another gracious and courageous friend has stepped into the arena to fight our battle. The article on this question, which appeared in The Herald on Saturday, is a momentous one, and will, undoubtedly, lead other sympathetic friends to do likewise and expose the injustice and wrongs under which my poor, helpless, downtrodden people are being hustled into an untimely grave.[56]

No sooner had the white man invaded our land than the extermination of our people began, and it has gone on, and is still going on, under various guises. It is an undeniable fact that the early colonists, not only dislodged our people from their hunting grounds, but, with the help of the police, shot down hundreds of them. It seems the police can do so still with impunity, although not going to the same measure of excess. Their wickedness in this respect knew no bounds; they armed and taught our men to go on a pleasure excursion occasionally, shooting down their own people for the squatters' rum and "bacca".

Attitude of whites

The whole attitude of the white man towards the aborigine has all along been to dis-spirit and humiliate him, to extinguish his self-respect, to suppress his ambition; in short, to kill his hope. To his natural disabilities the white man has added other disabilities which I cannot enlarge upon here, and which make the conditions of life seem so hard that the very atmosphere in which he lives appears hostile, and the consequence is he has no will to live.

Our so-called protectors are diligently attending to the care of my people, with the full conviction that they are slowly but surely passing out. "Let us", say they, "make them as comfortable as we can before they pass out". Hence all their efforts for the care of my people are mere palliatives, only sop. There is absolutely nothing, as a matter of fact, in all their activities, feeding, clothing, housing and caring, which can be counted as of vital interest to lift us up by education and other means to aspire to the dignity of citizenship. Other colored races in Fiji, New Zealand, Samoa, New Hebrides have been raised to the dignity of teachers, lawyers, doctors and clergymen.

The mentality of my people, according to the late Sir Baldwin Spencer, the greatest authority on this question, is not inferior to the white man's.[57] While the efforts put forth for the advance of the colored people, I have just mentioned have been attended with success, because they have been carried on with confidence, earnestness and assiduity, there have been no serious attempts for our advancement in Australia.

The race changing

Do not think of the future fitness of the aborigines to improve intellectually, socially and morality in terms of the past. The aborigines of today are different from those of yesterday. They are more industrious, more ambitious, more intellectual, more provident and less vicious. They are eagerly but patiently waiting for the time to come when the white people now occupying our land and enjoying the inestimable benefits it yields (I mean the white people in power, who are still possessed of a live conscience) will shake off their indifference and heartlessness and wholeheartedly arise to give our cause the hearing and consideration it deserves. We are the descendants of the people you have unjustly disinherited of their land, and of their privileges.

We are not unreasonable in asking you to secure for us the best prospects of free development and to provide for us a full opportunity to display our capacities, and so legislate that we should know that we live and move and have our being in Australia as right, not on sufferance. We are at present — shame on the Governments of this land — landless and homeless wanderers. — We ask you to secure land and homes for us by public law and not by regulation of the Aboriginal Protection Board.

Native M.P. wanted

As one who thoroughly knows his people, their thoughts and feelings, their likes and dislikes, I may be privileged to suggest that the aborigines should be placed under the supervision of the Federal Government. They should have a native representative in Federal Parliament and a native protector with an advisory council comprising whites and aborigines in each State.

We strongly deprecate the policy of placing us under the supervision of the police. Many of my people shun the aboriginal stations controlled by the Aborigines' Protection Boards because of this and its gaol-like conditions. Police and gaol are inseparables in the mind of an aborigine, and this association does not tend to elevate, but depress him.

8. William Cooper, 'Treatment of Aborigines', letter to the Editor, *Age*, 16 March 1933

I desire to draw attention to the inhuman treatment of aborigines in Central Australia. These aborigines live under primitive conditions. But they are not allowed to live in peace. White men who call themselves civilised, go among them with firearms, and often use them on unarmed aborigines. Aborigines have a right to receive the utmost consideration and best of attention from the whites. They lost much when the whites came to Australia, and surely it is the duty of whites to protect them from attacks by armed men.

We read in newspapers of 3rd February, 1933, of a grave charge against the police for alleged acts of brutality against aborigines. These charges were made by Mr R. S. Schenck, of the Mount Margaret Aboriginal Mission Station, Morgan, W.A. He stated that for no apparent reason members of the police force shot natives down. It is the duty of the Government and all white people to take up this matter, and to provide tribal sanctuaries for the aborigines. It is against the nature of the aborigine to move from his home country and he should be well cared for in his natural environment. If carefully educated in right surroundings aborigines would soon accustom themselves to the ways of decent white men. Scientists, anthropologists and sociologists are doing nothing to bring about just conditions for these aborigines, but simply look upon them as material for investigation and experiment. During the war many aborigines were among the first to offer for enlistment in the A.I.F. to protect the British Empire. Surely, then, it is our duty to protect the remainder of their race from inhuman treatment.

When the first white settlers arrived 145 years ago there were hundreds of thousands of aborigines here. But brutal extermination followed, and the number of full-blooded natives was reduced to 17,000. The killing of natives is continuing to-day, and if it is not soon stopped the Australian aborigine will become extinct.

Of course, all whites are not destroyers of natives. And not all whites give no consideration to them. There are many, for instance missionary workers, who go into the unpleasant parts of Australia to assist the natives. They suffer many tortures and inconveniences, but, realising the duty of the white race to the natives, they continue their work uncomplainingly. They who devote their lives to the preservation and uplift of the aborigines will be remembered forever, and given a honored place in the history books of the future. Surely, then, it is the duty of every white person in Australia to follow their example. Of course, all cannot go into Central Australia, but all of us can bring pressure to bear on the Government to have the aborigines protected from armed men, and to provide sanctuaries in the areas in which they now live. — Yours, &c.

9. W. Cooper to the Board of Protection for Aborigines, Victoria [September 1933?]

On behalf of my people I have The honour to most humbly approach you. Seeking your permission to send to, and have signed by the Aboriginal population under your Charge, the undermention petition a Copy of which is to be forwarded to His Majesty King George V. of England asking him on our behalf to do his utmost in taking suitable steps in preventing the extinction of the Aborigines race. Obtaining better conditions for all. Obtaining Power to propose a Member of Parliament to be Chosen by My People to represent them in the Federal Parliament.

Trusting that my humble request will receivery every Consideration. I have the Honour to be yours sir obediently

10. *Herald* (Melbourne), 15 September 1933, 'M.H.R. for Natives: King to Be Petitioned: Unique Move'

Australia's native race — the aborigines — is taking steps for the first time in its history to secure from the King representation in the Federal Parliament. This is demanded as a right in a petition which is being circulated for signatures.

Some people of aboriginal blood are interesting themselves in the move, and much of the initial work is falling to the lot of Mr William Cooper, of Ballarat Road, Footscray, who said today that the object was to place the aborigines on the same footing as the Maoris. In New Zealand, he said, Parliamentary and Government offices were open to Maoris equally with Europeans.

Extracts from the petition as it will later be presented to the authorities are as follows ...

Mr Cooper will seek the signatures of aborigines and half-castes at mission stations. Even without these he hopes to secure about 600.

11. Petition to King George V

PETITION of the Aboriginal Inhabitants of Australia to His Majesty, King George V, by the Grace of God, of Great Britain, Ireland, and British Dominions beyond the seas, King; Defender of the Faith; Emperor of India.

TO THE KING'S MOST EXCELLENT MAJESTY, IN COUNCIL THE HUMBLE PETITION of the undersigned Aboriginal inhabitants of the Continent of Australia respectfully sheweth: —

THAT WHEREAS it was not only a moral duty, but a strict injunction, included in the commission issued to those who came to people Australia, that the original inhabitants and their heirs and successors should be adequately cared for;

AND WHEREAS the terms of the commission have not been adhered to in that —
(a) Our lands have been expropriated by Your Majesty's Governments, and
(b) Legal status is denied to us by Your Majesty's Governments;
AND WHEREAS all petitions made on our behalf to Your Majesty's Governments have failed.
YOUR PETITIONERS humbly pray that Your Majesty will intervene on our behalf, and, through the instrument of Your Majesty's Governments in the Commonwealth of Australia —
will prevent the extinction of the Aboriginal race and give better conditions for all, granting us the power to propose a member of parliament, of our own blood or a white man known to have studied our needs and to be in sympathy with our race, to represent us in the Federal Parliament.
AND YOUR PETITIONERS WILL EVER PRAY.

12. *Cinesound Review*, no. 100, 29 September 1933, 'Australian Royalty Pleads for His People: Burraga, chief of Aboriginal Thirroul tribe, to petition the King for blacks' representation in Federal Parliament'

Before the white man set foot in Australia, my ancestors were as Kings in their own right. And I, Aboriginal chief Burraga, am a direct descendant of the royal line.

The black man sticks to his brethren, and always keeps the rules which were laid down before the white man put foot upon these shores. One of the greatest laws amongst the Aboriginals was to love one another. And they always kept it in law. Where will you find a white man or a white woman today that will say "I love my neighbour". It quite amuses me to hear people saying "I don't like the black man". But he's damn glad to live in a black man's country all the same!

I am calling a corroboree of all the natives of New South Wales to send a petition to the King, in an endeavour to improve our condition. All the black man wants is representation in Federal Parliament. There is also plenty fish in the river for us all, and land to grow all we want. One hundred and fifty years ago the Aboriginals owned Australia, and today he demands more than the white man's charity. He wants the right to live!

13. William Cooper to the Prime Minister of Australia, Joseph Lyons, 23 October 1933

I would like to draw your attention to the splended action of a Sister Colony of our Empire, the Governing Powers having seen fit to provide ways and means to preserve the Eskimo Race. Surely some consideration can be given to our own Race here, to prevent their extinction and so help hold up the dignity of the British Empire.

A Petition similar to the enclosed has been forwarded on to Sydney, South Australia, Queensland, Perth and Victoria Boards for Protection of Aborigines, and the following have replied viz. — Sydney. Referred to Commonwealth Government. South Aust. The wards have permission to sign. Brisbane. Has refused permission to get signatures. Victoria. Have forwarded to Manager of Lake Tyres [Tyers] and West. Australia have not replied.

These results are very disjointed and unsatisfactory thus leaving it for me to approach you with my appeal.

I have the Honour to remain,
Sir,
Yours obediently

14. William Cooper to Rev. E. R. B. Gribble, 26 October 1933

Your most kind letter reach me safly to day. and no need to say how pleased I was to received it, it is the first letter I have rec'd of the Kind, and I feel sure I am going to get on alright, now you are Taking part in this good Cause, There are many more. I am sure will help in that Part of this Continent. that you are aquainted with, now I will tell you a little of my work in Correspondence with one and a-nother, first Called a meeting with my Native people to Disgusse [i.e. discuss] about aranging a petition to be forwarded to his Majesty King George V, and we unanimously decided to Carrie on with it, my first step was to write to the Aboriginal protection Boards in the five states, replys received as follows Queensland refuses south Australia give permission to all Aborigines to sign any petition they wish to, Victoria very stubborn. Copy of my letter was forwarded to Lake Tyers Mission for consideration, and again wrote to the Board and no answere, I was compelled to appoint one of the members to see the Board on our behalf, so I should be getting a reply next week, N.S. Wales forwarded a Copy of my letter to the Commonwealth Government also for Consideration, west Australia no reply, I have written to the Prime Minister seeking for a definit reply from all Boards, when I receive the reply from the Prime Minister I shall send on[.] we must keep in close touch with each other till the Petition is Completed, you will please find inclose a Copy of the Petition, and no need to tell you what to do with the Petition as you will know Better with it. it is the Duty of Every man and women with Aboriginal Blood in them over the age of 20 years to signe the Petition, and I hope my people will not fail to signe, and help all they can that we may get improvement in our Conditions, I may say if you wish to take Copy of the Petition in Closed you are at liberty to do so, to send to some of your aquaintance in that part of the continent, I am adressing this letter

to the adress I sent to befor, so, when your answering give me your adress again,
I am trusting to receive some more good information from you.
Closing with kindest regards to all my Aboriginal friends,
Not forgetting you
I am your
faithfull
Friend
P.S. to avoid weight in letter I am not send the forms as I trust you will arange them

15. William Cooper to Rev. E. R. B. Gribble, 31 October 1933

I am Pleased to have receive the Book safly and in order, I have not had time to have a read it as you know I have so Much Writing [to] do at Present, hope to start with it next week, I am sorry to say I have not received any reply from any of the Members up to now, in the Event of me not getting a reply within a few day, what would you suggest in doing in this Matter, I will be glad to receive any information you wish to suggest to me, as I want all the help I can get in this Great work I have taken on, I did not get any sympathy from any of the Church people here in Melbourne. The Government and our Christian People are very dull on this question, I am at a lost to know why. as I am sure they know their responsibility for the Aboriginal people, the Aboriginals are men women and Children and same as we are in Gods sight, God [h]as made us after his own image and Left with us the fear of himself, the same as he did with the White races, and if Everyman had the same respect as you have for [the] Aboriginal race there would be no sufferage for their race of People, I feel sorry for my People that have got in Contact with the worst side of Civilisation that has bought to them Corruption and Diseases which is a problem at self for these people to get rid of, I have a longing to be near you. I feel sure you would be a great help to me in this good Cause Which I have taken on. my education is not what I would like it to be, it seems a struggle to me to keep up to the standard I have got the worke up to, but all the same I am sticking to it to the end, I wrote to rev. J. Noble some months ago and have not received any reply from him, I would liked to have got in touch with him, he may have been a good help to me. I received a letter from one of my friends in Western Australia who has kindly offered to help me in getting signatures, I have forwarded a copy of the Petition, also received another from Mr Craig at Cairns giving me a helping hand, I have also sent a Copy of the Petition to him. I have received a list of names from South Australia about 160, and I should soon be getting a number of others in a few days now — I have not been home for some time but hope to go home at Xmas time, and will remember you to Boby Cooper, I am sure we would like to see you, so if you should have the Luck to come our way dont forget to give us a call.

Now Mr Gribble I thing [i.e. think] I shall draw to a close with kindest regards to you & your family.

I beg to remain yours faithfull friend

16. William Cooper to the Minister for the Interior, J. A. Perkins, 13 January 1934

On behalf of the members of my race, I'm exceedingly pleased to convey to you, our commendation for the action and stand you have taken, and valuable suggestions for the relief of the Aborigines and half-castes; also, the report of half-caste girls who have had such good instruction, and by their citizenship proves and dispels the idea, that no good could come of training them to white peoples custom and habits.

The arrangement of Married Police protectors is a step in the right direction, yet, we think if a Separate body of protectors be appointed (Married by All means) who have been properly instructed to win the confidence of the pure Aborigine, greater results and more relations would be established as a native is naturally antagonistic to Officialdom a Police protector always carries, even if he has not got any uniform on when in touch with them, this is one thing to be avoided, to prove to them the Honesty of the Government instructions, as the Aboriginal is very quick in observation.

Yours Respectfully

17. William Cooper to Mr A. E. Parker, 17 March 1934

Would it be Possible to get Premission from you for a Visit to Corranderrk on saturday staying there one night with W. Russell. my object is to speak to them of Aboriginal afairs. trusting to receive a successful reply. I am yours faithfully

P.S. Visit shall be saturday 24/3/34

18. William Cooper to H. Makin, MHR, 19 March 1934

Why can't Mr Bleakley give me something definite, as regards my petitioning my own people for signatures in Queensland, as each of the other States have done, it is just upon six months since I first applied, & the enquiries of the attitude of the other States are still being put forward as the reason, Surely it does not take all that time to get an answer, other matters of less importance get more business action than this has, the whole matter is being held up, as my people do not want to do anything against the Board of Protection, yet are willing to sign so long as it will not offend.

If something decisive is not arrived at very soon, greater publicity will be given to the unnecessary delay meted out by the Board, their duty is to help our race in a reasonable manner, as we are subjects of the Realm.

In your reply dated 4 Dec 33 you suggest that if there is any objection raised, to apply to yourself or some other Member, will you please accept my appeal & try & help me, Thanking you in anticipation.

Yours Respectfully

19. William Cooper to the Minister for the Interior, J. A. Perkins, 7 May 1934

It is proposed that a deputation, composed of one representative of the Aboriginal race from each State, should wait upon the Commonwealth Government in September next, with the object of securing some amelioration of the conditions under which the native people are at present living.

I respectfully beg to be informed whether it will be possible for free railway transport to be provided for the members of the deputation, whose names and places of residence are as follow:

W.A.   Mr N.C. Harris, Wongan Hills.
S.A.   Mr W. Taylor, Port Victoria.
Vic.   Mr W. Cooper, Melbourne.
N.S.W. (not yet appointed.)
Qld.   Mr Jas Noble, Palm Islands.

Thanking you in anticipation of your consideration and reply, I am Sir, Yours respectfully

20. William Cooper to the Prime Minister, Joseph Lyons, 20 June 1934

As it is the intention to present a Deputation consisting of a Representative from each State of the Aboriginal Races, sometime during November next, to wait upon the Federal Parliament to proffer their petition to appeal for more amelioration and better conditions than those existing, as, the very hard treatment some are receiving, which only causes bitter feeling and a desire to do something desperate in spite, and so increase greater difficulties to overcome before a proper understanding can be gained.

Would you, as Premier arrange for a free pass of transport for one representative from each State to the Federal Parliament, as they have no other means by which they can get there. I may state that Dr Maloney is in support of my application for this assistance.

Trusting that my humble request will receive every consideration, I have the honour to be, Yours obediently

21. William Cooper to the Prime Minister, Joseph Lyons, 28 July 1934

In view of the approaching Federal Election, I am writing to ask for your views, concerning the representation of my people in Parliament. If returned to Parliament will you do your best to further the cause. The Maories of N.Z. have had Parliament representation since 1867. There for the Parliamentary representation of the Aborigines of Australia is long overdue. Trusting to receive an Early reply, I am Sir, Yours Obediently

22. William Cooper to the Prime Minister, Joseph Lyons, 20 August 1934

As I have had no definite reply to my previous letter, probably, owing to you being fully occupied by the intense interest you are taking in the Federal Election, thus, my appeal may be overlooked.

However, would you be good enough to take a suggestion from me, as I think it will be of vital interest to you as well as my people especially as the subject has been so prominently brought before the public, even as late as Saturday 18th instant in the "Herald" by Mr W. F. [i.e. D. F.] Thomson, "My Three Years in the Stone Age", pointing out the real necessity of doing something to help pay the Aborigines for the loss of facilities to live properly, without the white population forcing themselves and having contact with them, provision could be arranged to their benefit, therefore by you referring to this matter in your policy that you will be advocating during your Election Tour.

Trusting due consideration will be given to my suggestion.

I remain Honourable Sir,

Yours respectfully

23. William Cooper to Rev. E. R. B. Gribble [September or October 1934]

You will be anxious to hear from me regarding the organising of our petition that is to be presented to the King.

The petition is in perfect order and we are getting along with it as well as we can expect. I am pleased to say I have now in hand, signatures amounting to 2,500 and we are expecting another 2,500 which should bring the total to about 6,000.

I am sorry to have kept you waiting so long but we have been held up all this time by the Government in not answering the letters I wrote to them. I may say that I have written to all the Railway Departments asking them to grant me five passes for five Aboriginal representatives to enable us to meet the Commonwealth Government at Canberra with a deputation for the purpose of asking the Government for better conditions before forwarding the petition to the King. I have been refused the passes so I am trying another Department which will take some time to put through.

However, we must keep on seeking for our rights. The election has been the main cause of all the delay and now the Centenary and the Melbourne Cup to be run in November. Then comes Christmas and New Year. All these will cause a lot of delay in our efforts so we will have to have patience.

We are getting along very well and there is nothing to be alarmed of. It is the duty of all our Natives to take part in some way in this great cause for the betterment of all our people.

With kindest regards,
From Yours faithfully

P.S. Deputation not aranged yet owing to Election Delays. I am sending these notes all a round to our suports.

24. Anna Morgan, 'Under the Black Flag', *Labor Call*, 20 September 1934

What flag flies over the Australian Aborigines? Some say it is the British flag. We say that we live under the Black Flag of the Aborigines "Protection" Board. We have not the same liberty as the white man, nor do we expect the same justice. For twelve years we lived on a mission station in New South Wales. My husband was given a 30-acre block of land; he cleared and fenced it, and then waited for implements to break it up. There were only two teams of horses to do all the work for ten such farms, and no assistance from outside was allowed. When at last we did get in a crop the Board took away the land from us. We wanted to remain on the land and make our living however we could. But, no; the Board would not have that; we must live on the mission station.

After the men had cleared and fenced about 90[0] acres of virgin soil the manager wrote to the Board, saying that the men were too lazy to work the land. Those who protested against this injustice were classed as agitators, an expulsion order was made out against them, and it was served by the local police. My husband was among the victims. Soon after, he went away, but because we had no way of removing our belongings, we left some at his father's place.

A few months later we came, prepared to take our belongings away. We stayed one night at his father's place, and the next day my husband got a summons for trespassing. He was taken and gaoled for fourteen days. Did he break any of the British laws? No. He broke the laws of the Black Flag. When a white man is charged with a crime, he is taken to court and judged. If innocent, he is allowed to go home to his family, and there the matter ends. A black man is expelled from the Mission — the land reserved for him and his people — and can never go back to his own people again. Perhaps the family, unwilling to be separated from him, shares his exile until it pleases the mighty "Protectors" of the aborigines, or their managers, to give them a gracious pardon, and allow them to return home again. My husband and I have been expelled for all time.

Here we are! Taken from the bush, placed in compounds, told, "This is your home and your children's as long as there is an aboriginal left"; put under managers, scarcely allowed to think for ourselves. We were suppressed.

We were half-educated. We lived on what white people call "sustenance." We bought our own clothes. We cleared Crown lands. At the age of fourteen our girls were sent to work — poor, illiterate, trustful little girls to be gulled by the promises of unscrupulous white men. We all know the consequences. But, of course, one of the functions of the Aborigines' Protection Board is to build a white Australia. Those who pride themselves on "British fair play" should think of us who live under the Black Flag. We want a home. We want education. You have taken our beautiful country from us — "a free gift."

Even a worm will turn, and we, the down-trodden of the earth, at last raise a feeble protest, and dare to ask for better conditions and the abolition of the rule of the "Black Flag." Will you help us?

25. Notes of deputation representing Aborigines and various associations interested in Aboriginal welfare to the Minister for the Interior, Thomas Paterson, Melbourne, 23 January 1935

...*Mr Cooper* presented the following statement which was read on his behalf by Mr James:

This deputation has the Honor to represent the aboriginal population of Australia.

We, on behalf of the descendants of the aborigines naturally are greatly concerned in everything effecting our people. We consider that it is one of the most pressing problems of the day, yet it does not seem to seriously trouble the mind of the Government.

Therefore, on behalf of the aboriginal population of Australia we appeal for a constructive policy with better conditions than those existing and under which our people have to live. We respectfully remind the Government that a strict injunction to the effect "that the aborigines and their descendants should be properly cared for" was included in the Commission issued to those who came overseas to Australia, and we trust the present Government will take every lawful means to extend the protection to the native population, who are His Majesty's subjects, and the Government must punish, with exemplary severity all acts of violence and injustice which may in manner be attempted or practiced against the aborigines who are to be considered as much under safeguard of the laws as the white people under the British Flag.

Believing the British Empire to stand for justice, order, freedom and good Government we pledge ourselves as citizens of the British Commonwealth of Australia to maintain the heritage handed down to us by the Creator which we believe to be true, and we, therefore, with confidence, desire moderation and forbearance to be exercised by all classes in their intercourse with native inhabitants, and that they will omit no opportunity of assisting to fulfil His Majesty's most gracious and benevolent intention to them by promoting advancement in civilization under the blessing of Divine Providence.

This injunction has not been carried into effect for our people have been driven further and further into the barren wastes on which it is impossible to live for much longer, consequently, the native people are faced with extinction.

Many of our civilised aborigines have not been given the status of citizens of the Commonwealth.

Many have no voice in its Government and no vote in the election of Parliament, and are apparently cut off from all opportunity of becoming good citizens and a valuable asset to the country.

I wish to point out having had 60 years' experience of a fruitless task and waste of good energy on an Aboriginal Settlement on which no useful industries have been given to enable them to become useful and independent of the support of the Government.

The aborigines should not be blamed because it is not their fault, but the fault of the policy pursued by the various Governments in not adopting the suggestions mentioned before.

The Maoris of New Zealand have had Parliamentary representations since 1867, therefore, the Parliamentary representation of the Australian aborigine is long overdue.

In view of these facts, we, on behalf of the native races of Australia, respectfully submit the following requests:

(1) That we be allowed aboriginal representatives to protect our interest in the State and Federal Parliaments;

(2) That a Federal Department of Native Affairs be established to unify the aboriginal work of all States so that Australia may work out a national policy for her native race;

(3) That a sympathetic officer be appointed for this Department to do for the aborigines what Sir Hubert Murray has done in New Guinea.

As, Sir, there are other speakers, I thank you for your patient hearing ...

Mr Douglas Nichols: Sir, I endorse the statements which have been made. Much more could be done for our people. They should have representation in Parliament. We need not be a hindrance. We could work together with the white men and we look to you, Sir, to help us...

Mrs A. Morgan: I speak on behalf of our native women. We need more education than we get with some of our Administrators. If we get the same education as the white girl we could stand alongside white people.

Mr James: The case of my people for more than 100 years has baffled all administrations. Protectors are appointed to dispense monies to the best advantage, and to feed, clothe and educate my people. Their work should be for our moral, social and intellectual advancement, but they have not lived up to their responsibilities. They have not done anything to raise the dignity of our people. We should have a say in the making of laws. Education is not systematically taught but a mutilated curriculum. Boys are drifting back. Teachers are unclassified and are not interested in the progress of our people.

There should be a suitable library to foster the love of reading. The system of today is pauperizing us and not helping us in any way. It should be altered to enable us to support ourselves and to have grants of land. There is plenty of land which can be split up and used. We should have a native representative in Parliament and a Protector in each State. We should be given opportunities such as are enjoyed by the aristocratic Brahman of India. We understand our people and strongly deprecate the policy of appointing policemen as administrators.

26. William Cooper, Real Australian Aboriginal Association, to the Minister for the Interior, Thomas Paterson, 1 April 1935

As a Big Game Hunt and study of Native Custom life and condition of the Aboriginals in their primitive state, is being arranged, personally conducted by motors, to Central Australia during the months of May June and July next.

It is hoped that the Government will take every Lawful means for the Protection and care of the Aboriginals during the Sportsman's hunting, and that nothing so callous as the wilful shooting at natives will take place while the expedition are enjoying themselves, and that those who are conducting the party, will be men who have been chosen to carry out their duties with integrity and fully conscious of their responsibility, as nothing so revolting revelation as was disclosed by Friday evenings "Herald" 29 Mch 1935, is desired.[58]

Trusting that all precaution will be fully maintained. I beg to remain, Yours Respectfully

27. William Cooper, Real Australian Native Association, to the Minister for the Interior, Thomas Paterson, 8 April 1935

On behalf of the Aborigines population of Australia from whom I have received 2000 signatures, from all parts of Australia authorising me to plead for justice; And noticing the continual reports in daily presses of ill treatment of Aborigines, reports of a similar nature have been coming from different parts of Australia. Fifty years to my knowledge. in my travels through Queensland, South Aust, N, S, Wales and Victoria, [I] have noticed large tribes of Aborigines, and to my estimation appeared hundreds of thousands. Turning to the general liberty of early history estimates millions of Aborigines, and it is publicly known the numbers reduced from Millions, to 70,000, aborigines all told. Sir, we humbly pray that you will intervene on our behalf through instrument of the Government in the

Commonwealth of Australia, to prevent the gold seekers, settlers, and others, from further ill treatment to Aborigines.

Trusting a favourable Consideration will be given to our requests, and your petitioners will ever pray.

I am,
Yours Sincerely

28. William Cooper, Secretary, Australian Aborigines' League, to Rev. E. R. B. Gribble [after 29 May 1935]

Dear friend I am send you a Copy of an answere I received from the minister for the interior of the Deputation which we waited on him on 23/1/35 you will notice it is only a tempreory one. there is further consideration to be given on this matter and I will write again. I will sending my son to N.T. to inspect the county [i.e. country] the Government is Granting to our people. I am anxious for you to tell me the Best way to get to it from here and if there is a man that could go to the Territory with my son to show him around. you May Know of a man in the Territory. and another question is [it] possible for you to reccomend a Aboriginal or a sympithtic white man to take the seat to represent our people in the N.T. if so let me know at your Earlyiest. all is Working well in our favour. the public oppinion is getting very powerfull here in Victoria.

I am now Closing
with Kindest regards
I am yours faithfully

29. William Cooper to Sir John Harris, Secretary, Anti-Slavery and Aborigines Protection Society, 19 July 1935

Having received a letter from Miss H. Baillie London this morning asking me to send a Copy of a letter which I received from Mr Paterson the Minister for the interior, the letter is a reply to our Deputation held on the 23/1/35. you will Notice on the letter a further Consideration, which we will receive about the End of the year. I feel sure you would know of the Cruelty the Aborigines of Australia have suffered. if you require any information in any way regards Aborigines affairs I Will only be to please to let you know. I may say some of the Natives in the western parts of this Continent are not receiving Justice they righty [i.e. rightly] Deserve this matter is a National one and concerns every respectable Person of the Britis Empire.

I will be anxiously waiting for a reply,
I am yours sincerely

30. William Cooper, Secretary, Australian Aborigines' League, to the Premier, New South Wales, Bertram Stevens, 19 February 1936

My organisation is deeply troubled and grieved over developments in Aboriginal control in New South Wales, at any rate at Cumeroogunja. For some years now, in addition to the regular rationing, unemployed dark men have been issued with a ration for themselves and their families. The ration was meagre, certainly, but it was eked out to maintain life though it could not prevent cases of malnutrition. Recently action has been taken at Cumeroogunja to stop the rations of all families of which the breadwinner was an able bodied man. These have been directed to seek employment.

At the moment seasonal occupation is available and the men are so engaged but this will soon pass and we can only see starvation ahead for our people. Already distress is evident which will be accentuated by the approach of winter. We appeal to you, at once, to direct that adequate rations be issued to all dark folk needing them. In other words, we ask for a reversion to the practice obtaining prior to the recent action. But we ask this more as a temporary measure.

Aboriginal natives, no matter what the state of their culture, are debarred by legislation from obtaining sustenance as granted to white unemployed, *and to dark unemployed here in Victoria* as well as to the whites. This we contend is unreasonable and unfair as well as being quite unchristian. We definitely ask that the dole be extended to the dark people where they are unemployed in the same conditions as applies to whites. We feel that our request is most reasonable.

We anticipate that the question of cost will be raised but whatever that may be will be offset by the ration not issued and the cost will be further offset by work done for the dole. We do quite definitely feel that we are entitled to reasonable comfort, merely from the fact that this land was ours, with assured living, before the whites came, but we do not want to stress that because we believe that the emancipation of our race will not come that way. It is our considered opinion that the dark man must be taught to be self-reliant and industrious and to win his rights by sheer worthiness. Work for the dole will do this. Men will be paid for work done and they will spend the money obtained to purchase necessities. If these can be purchased from the depot at the station when a native is resident on one, this would be preferable to their having to go to a privately kept store. Those not living on a station would of course purchase their goods in the usual way.

The second matter is causing deep perturbation and even grief to the mothers. It is reported that, consequent on a visit of high officials to Cumeroogunja many of the young girls, some as tender in years as 13, have been compulsorily taken from their homes and, in some cases sent to situations, which they report are very hard. (It is quite realised that this may merely be because of the inexperience of the girls). Other girls, who have not had any training, are being sent to Cootamundra, which our people regard with dread as in the nature of a gaol. I have no very certain information as to the definite particulars of this complaint but you will have full details.

I would request, Sir, that you go personally into these two matters and that you deal with them with a kindliness our race has not experienced.

Trusting to hear from you in reply at a very early date and hoping your communication will be of the nature of good news, I have the Honor to be, Your obedient servant

31. William Cooper, Secretary, Australian Aborigines' League, to the Hon. the Minister for the Interior, 22 February 1936

Australian Aborigines' League Constitution

1. *Name:* THE Name of the League shall be the "AUSTRALIAN ABORIGINES' LEAGUE".

2. *Membership:* Membership shall be either Full or Associate.

Full Full Membership shall only be open to persons possessing some degree of aboriginal blood. Any person who has attained the age of 18 years and is fully or partly of aboriginal descent may register as a member. Those under 18 years may register as Junior Full members.

Associate Any person, other than an aboriginal native, who is sympathetic with the Aims of the League may register as an Associate Member.

Life Membership Membership, for life, Full or Associate, may be granted on the payment of One Pound (£1) toward the Funds of the League.

Honorary Life Membership Honorary Life Membership, for services rendered, may be granted at the pleasure of the Executive of the League.

3. *Badge* Any member, Full or Associate, shall be entitled to wear any badge which may be adopted by the League.

The Badge of the League shall be sold to members, full or associate, at a price to be determined, but, at the discretion of the Executive Committee, a badge may be given to any person who, in the opinion of the Executive, should be so recognized.

4. *Officials* While the administrative positions in the League should primarily be filled by full members, it shall be competent for Associate members to be appointed to any position.

5. *Contributions* Excepting for Junior Full members, whose annual contribution fee shall be sixpence (6d) the annual fee for membership shall be One Shilling, for either Full or Associate Membership, to be payable in

advance. It shall be competent for the Executive to admit aboriginals to full membership without such charge if this course is justified.

6. *Annual Meeting* The Annual Meeting of the League shall be held, if possible, in the month of November each year, on a date to be arranged by the Executive. At this meeting the occupancy of all offices shall be considered. At this meeting the Treasurer shall present a statement of receipts and expenditure, duly audited.

7. *Objects* The Objects of the League shall be to cooperate with any Organization working for the promotion of a national policy, or for the amelioration of the disabilities of aboriginal natives of Australia or to make representations as may be necessary to promote the well-being of the said natives.

The ultimate object of the League shall be the conservation of special features of Aboriginal culture and the removal of all disabilities, political, social or economic, now or in future borne by aboriginals and to secure their uplift to the full culture of the British race.

8. *Immediate Programme* The immediate programme of the League shall be the progressive elevation of the aboriginal race by education and training in the arts and crafts of European culture in the manner as set forth hereunder:

For primitive aborigines

Until such time as the primitive aborigines are civilised, and while living in their primitive state, to secure the unalienable possession of adequate reserves, to which white men shall only have access by the authority of the Chief Protector of Aboriginal Natives.

Offences by white men against aboriginal natives to be punishable by similar penalties to those inflicted for like offences against white men.

The establishment of special Courts of Justice for the trial of native prisoners in which the recognition of Aboriginal tribal laws and customs as complementary to the laws of the land shall be given effect to.

Full sustenance to be ensured to all natives.

Progressive civilisation of the young people by the medium of education, including Industrial Training.

For the semi-civilised and de-tribalised natives

The provision of reserves of land suitable for stock, agriculture or other farming, with adequate machinery, equipment and training, to be unalienable and to which white men shall have access only by the authority of the Chief Protector of Aboriginal natives.

The safeguarding of the interests of aboriginal natives who may be in the service of white men.

The right to work for adequate remuneration or the provision of full rations and housing for aboriginal natives of both sexes.

Invalid or Old Age Pensions, or their equivalent in rations and housing to be available to all aboriginal natives similarly as to white people. No aboriginal who is living privately can be compelled to return to a settlement before becoming entitled to this provision, unless in special circumstances, as may be decided by the Chief Protector of Aboriginal Natives.

Free education in State Schools or the provision of special schools, with qualified teachers, for native children: Scholars to be encouraged to qualify up to the standard of White education. High Schools or secondary colleges to be available to aboriginal children qualifying to enter same or the provision of special schools in which shall be provided the same privileges as obtained in similar schools for white children. Education to include technical training.

Legal protection for natives. Punishment of offenders to be rigorously enforced as in the case of offences against white people.

For civilised natives

The provision of allotments of land suitable for agriculture or other farming, with requisite machinery and equipment, to be available to natives to work for their own profit. Such land to be unalienable property of the native concerned, and to be disposable by Will to the next of kin of the native concerned.

The right to work for adequate remuneration or the provision of full rations and housing for aboriginal natives of both sexes.

Invalid or Old-Age pensions, or their equivalent in rations and housing, to be available to all aboriginal natives similarly as to white people. No aboriginal who is living privately to be compelled to return to a settlement before becoming entitled to this provision, unless in special circumstances, as may be decided by the Chief Protector of Natives.

Free education in State Schools or the provision of special schools, with qualified teachers, for native children: Scholars to be encouraged to qualify up to the standard of the White education. High Schools or Secondary Colleges to be available to aboriginal children qualifying to enter same or the provision of special schools in which shall be provided the same privileges as obtained in similar schools for white children. Education to include technical training.

Full political, social and economic rights to be available, including the Franchise and eligibility for maternity bonus.

Legal protection for natives. Punishment of offenders to be rigorously enforced as in the case of offenders against white people.

Amendment Of Constitution

Additions and alterations to this Constitution may only be made at the Annual General Meeting, or at any Special Meeting called for that purpose, and of which due notice shall be given.

32. William Cooper, Secretary, Australian Aborigines' League, to N. M. Morley, 7 March 1936

We feel that it is our duty to draw the attention of people to the undisputable neglect of the Aborigines and the unsatisfactory conditions under which they exist.

We the descendants, who are educated and cultured to some extent, now become deeply concerned with the hardships and the disabilities of our defenceless primitive people, the most pitiful on earth who lived in a forest in peace and quietness before civilisation for thousands of years and when the early comers came here from overseas there was no consideration for the Aboriginals, neither did they realise the extent to which trade was responsible for the development of civilisation which apparently was, and still is, passing the original owners of the land.

We still find people who are so apt, with their British sense of superiority to look down on us of another colour, whereas they should make themselves friendly, sociable and give credit for the fine qualities which the Aborigines possess. They were people of very high standard of moral character until they came in contact with the worst side of civilisation.

One of the greatest qualities ever shown in history was when at least one thousand Aborigines enlisted to take part in the World's War from 1914 to 1918 for the protection of the British Empire for which they gave the supreme sacrifice and unfortunately received no better consideration for their valuable services at that war. It is now the duty of every level minded person to take up this great cause for the protection of the Native people, who are His majesty's subjects, and should be considered as much under the safeguard of the Law as any other man and equally entitled to the privileges of British subjects. People who are deeply concerned about the Aboriginals should help to bring pressure to remove all hardships of our less fortunate brothers and sisters and to uplift them morally, socially, intellectually and spiritually.

The ultimate object of our League shall be the conservation of special features of the Aboriginals culture and the removal of all hardships Political, social or economic.

I now take the liberty of presenting our Compliments by forwarding a copy of the constitution of our League and I am again seeking your urgent assistance for the help of the Australian Aborigines throughout the Continent, to afford them every protection and facilities for their future well being, as this is a movement of National interest and behoves every citizen to aid their less fortunate brethren in our serious plight. I am in hopes you will, to the utmost, give our serious plight every consideration for the betterment of this weak race.

Yours sincerely

33. *Argus,* 17 April 1936, 'Aborigines' Plea: Unhappy since Batman's Day'

Pathetic appeals for assistance for their people were made last night by aborigines at a meeting called to arrange the co-ordination of aboriginal amelioration organisations. They asked that something should be done so that their children and grandchildren should not have to suffer the disabilities and indignities they had had to undergo. The meeting was attended by a number of half-caste aborigines and many children. Douglas Nicholls, the League footballer, and Lynch Cooper, the Stawell Gift runner, were both present. Several of the aborigines sang corroboree choruses.

Mr W. Cooper said that his people felt themselves strangers within the gates of civilisation. White people seemed to care little whether they starved, and they generally gave to the aborigines the worst of civilisation instead of the best.

Speaking very diffidently Mrs M. Tucker, who came from the Moama Station, said that her people had a few real sympathisers. "We have not been happy since the days of Batman", she said; "we are sullen and oppressed through no fault of our own. We do not object to being nursemaids, servants, and washerwomen, but we would like our girls to learn a little more than that. We would like to learn the games white girls play. We are not angels, I know; but we are human and would like to be treated as such. I am glad that I am black and that the bruises one of my mistresses put on me never showed"…

Resolutions were passed urging that arrangements should be made for proper educational facilities for all aborigines, and that they should have full civic rights and legislative representation.

34. William Cooper, Secretary, Australian Aborigines' League, to the Minister for the Interior, Thomas Paterson, 15 June 1936

The attention of our League has been drawn to the staging of an aboriginal corroboree at Darwin for the benefit of American Tourists.

It is our opinion that the commercialising of the aboriginal people in this way is derogatory to the cause of their uplift, causing on the part of partly civilised people, a resuscitation of undesirable practices which will retard their uplift.

Our League does desire the preservation of the best features of aboriginal culture and feels that the preservation of certain corroboree dances, in the way the Old World peoples have retained their folk dances, is in harmony with this, but great care should be exercised till such time as the native race is so fully civilized that the outlook on the corroboree is just that of the Old World civilization on their folk dances.

We request that you will give instruction that no further instance be allowed to take place.

Thank you, Yours Sincerely

35. A. P. A. Burdeu, President, Australian Aborigines' League, to Rev. William Morley, Secretary, Association for the Protection of Native Races, 19 June 1936

Mr Cooper has just called to see me. We talked over the matter of the petition for which he has, so he informs me, about 2000 names. These are from all over Australia and ought [to] be far greater in number but for the fact that certain natives were afraid to sign, notwithstanding that the managers assured them that it was quite allowable. They felt there was a catch in it. The 2000 are on several lists which Mr Cooper and his son are pasting one under the other to make a roll of signatures under the petition. This should be ready very shortly.

I said to him that merely to send the petition to the Military Secretary to the Governor General may mean that the latter might not see it at all. Previously I had communicated with him as to the procedure and, in a not too courteous letter, he replied that the question of forwarding or not was a matter for the Governor-General's advisors to decide. His reply was not encouraging and I could quite contemplate that the petition might be sent to the Prime Minister's Dept. or to the Crown Solicitor's office and it might not only be not seen by the Governor General but it might not get away or be replied to by someone in Canberra. I asked Mr Cooper if he were willing to go to Canberra himself and suggested that you, for preference, or some member of the A.P.N.R. might go with him to Canberra there to present the document personally in a deputation to be introduced by one of the Federal members. I explained that you would know all the ropes and the weight of the A.P.N.R. behind the document would certainly ensure a good hearing.

I think I could ensure the expenses for you from Sydney and, of course, we would have to meet Mr Cooper's. In any case we would also have to be responsible for yours too if necessary.

Please just think it over and, if necessary, submit it to your executive, letting me know in good time as convenient to you as to what you think. We will know the value of your advice.

With best wishes,
Yours sincerely

36. William Cooper, Secretary, Australian Aborigines' League, to the Prime Minister, Joseph Lyons, 22 July 1936

The aborigines are looking forward with deep concern to the forthcoming conference of Premiers in Adelaide next month as they feel that their destinies are somewhat involved.

You have undertaken to bring the matter of aboriginal control and policy to the conference and we do plead that no circumstance be permitted to shelve or delay the matter.

We do plead for one controlling authority, the Commonwealth and request that all aboriginal interests be absolutely federalised. This will enable a continuous common policy of uplift, which we trust will contain provision for the exploitation of all natives' reserves by the natives. By the natives, under able leadership, and for the natives. We submit an aim, which is practicable, and that should be the ultimate self liquidation of the whole problem of uplift. So far from the aboriginal continuing to be a charge on the community, he can be made under sound and capable direction to be an asset to the community. This is a long vision no doubt.

We plead for this, but if the Premiers are not willing to lose a responsibility they do not wish to retain we plead for a common policy under Commonwealth control or influence with a subsidising of the States on the aboriginal per capita basis. We have no hope where the States with large aboriginal populations cannot adequately finance their obligations and the States with small aboriginal populations, or none, as in the case of Tasmania, should not be freed from responsibility.

We would request that the request of this League for parliamentary representation be considered. If the whole control is federalised this should be readily concedable, but if the States retain control, we submit that such representation should be accorded to our people in the States' legislature, at any rate where the aboriginal populations are numerous.

Trusting that you will bring these requests to the notice of the Premiers ...
I remain,
Yours respectfully

37. William Cooper, Secretary, Australian Aborigines' League, to the Minister for the Interior, Thomas Paterson, 31 October 1936

I have been instructed by the Executive of the Australian Aborigines' League to write to you thanking you for your earnest and valuable interest and the suggestions made by you, as appearing in the Press, on behalf of the aboriginal people of Australia.

For some years now, in fact from the time of the apprehension trial and acquittal of Tuckiar on the charge of murder, it has been daily evident that the sun of the Aboriginals' Cause is rising. We have been encouraged as we saw the steadily improving outlook and I have been personally heartened at the thought that, though now somewhat aged, I will see the emancipation of my people an assured thing.

I hope, and indeed, believe that the administration of which you are a member will go down to Aboriginal posterity as the emancipators of our race. May God guide you in the days ahead.

We feel it but right that our people should be the responsibility of the Federal Administration and we learn with delight from public statements that at least some of the States, South Australia and Western Australia as cases in point, are prepared to hand over their responsibilities to the Commonwealth. We know that the Commonwealth can discharge its responsibilities and we appreciate that the States cannot for the reason that where the white population is relatively smallest the dark population is largest while in the States with a large and wealthy white population the number of aboriginals is comparatively small: thus the bigger the need, the smaller the capacity to meet it.

For now over 100 years we have had experience of the waste of energy and loss of aboriginal lives through neglect. Our cause will not be neglected further if the Commonwealth assumes the responsibility. This is our hope and pleading.

At this time, so fraught with import to us, we feel that we must raise our voice in constructive appeal and we do request that the most careful attention be given to our requests. The forthcoming meeting of Chief Protectors and experts is well aware of the substance of our claims but we take the opportunity of again outlining our opinions:

1. Full Bloods and Half-castes

We would emphasise the fact that the full bloods are the descendants of the original owners of Australia. They are the lineal descendants of their fathers. The change in ownership by conquest should not invalidate their title to reasonable part of those lands and these rights should be admitted without cavil. I am sure that they are and only emphasise the point because it seems to be current opinion that half-castes have special rights as against the full blood and there is official discrimination against which we are ever in protest.

The half-caste is the descendent of the aboriginal and therefore joint heirs with the full blood. They are also descendents of the white man and thus heirs with the white race of all the rights of British nationhood.

Disregarding the matter of the mergence of the half-caste with either race, we disclaim acquiescence with current opinion and feel that, at any rate for a long time, the half-caste problem will continue to be present. We stress the real humanity of each section and our claims are based on that fact. To the extent that there has been discrimination in the past or the advantage of one section without regard to the other, we are in protest. We claim for each section the full rights of British nationality.

2. Capabilities of Aboriginals

The question of the uplift of the whole aboriginal population to full European culture depends on the capabilities of the race to assimilate that culture. We claim that it has been fully demonstrated that aboriginals of both full blood and mixed blood can do anything a white man is able to do. We further believe that the aboriginal must be a partner in this own uplift. Certainly expert guidance will be necessary, but, apart from that, he must "work out his own salvation". This is in the interests of the aboriginal himself and he is not seeking anything else than the right to obtain what he proves himself to be entitled to by his capacity to use it. Emancipation must come by the way of full manhood.

We have not produced doctors, lawyers and other professional leaders merely from the lack of the opportunity given to other colored races. We have produced practical men of varied experience as seamen, including masters, shearers with both gun and hand shears, wool classers, agriculturalists with expert knowledge of all farming operations, orchardists, millhands, motor and machinery experts, horse breakers. We have among our ranks those who have made good as squatters. We have public speakers, preachers, teachers and we claim that what has been done in the past can be again done by those yet uncultured. We are not insensible of the task but we would urge that civilisation has been acquired in the past merely by picking it up and the process took about three generations. We feel sure that an ordered plan of uplift, carefully and sympathetically applied must be more successful than the haphazard method or want of method.

3. Settlements

We feel that the comparative smallness of the numbers of aboriginals in the Southern portion of the Commonwealth and the considerable number in the Northern and Central areas constitutes two definite problems with quite different solutions.

Southern Aboriginals

The small number of aboriginals associated with the large white population introduces the economic disadvantage of color. In the years of depression it was found that preference to whites brought the dark race to extreme poverty. The usual avenue of employment for colored people is generally seasonal work. With the closing of the normal avenues of the White, the normal avenue of colored opportunity was taken. While this condition is now adjusting itself, the possibility of recurrence must always be borne in mind. Coupled with the fact that, in most cases, the sustenance for white unemployed was not available for dark persons, a continuance of the practice of having settlements for dark persons must continue. Men should be encouraged to compete in the general labor market and thus to live outside these settlements but in times of adversity or unemployment, the asylum in the settlement should be kept open. When illness or increasing age renders a person incapable of labor, the privilege of return to the settlement should be open. We claim that this should be voluntary and not compulsory and to make this possible we urge [that] full citizenship rights [such] as dole, Old Age or Invalid pensions, etc. should be available to dark and fair alike. This should apply also in settlements and from these allowances the dark folk should purchase their necessities instead of being given an issue of rations.

We feel that the policy of small settlements is not the best and the value of the community services, shopping facilities, garage etc. being given by aboriginals for aboriginals will be no small factor in uplift. At present community services are generally in the hands of white people, in cases tending to exploitation of the dark people and developing an inferiority complex.

The closed smaller settlements should not be expropriated but should be cut up for closer settlement farms, etc. for colored people.

Northern and Central Aboriginals

We submit that a practical ideal should be "the development of the North and Centre by Colored Australians instead of the proposed immigration of Nordic peoples and Southern Europeans. The policy of settlements is essential for training purposes and, to the extent that the aboriginal is a worker for wages, to be a base of operations. All settlements should be worked under expert supervision and on a commercial basis.

The aboriginal is most loyal to the person of the King and His administration. It will be seen that, to the extent that the aboriginal is used in the peopling of the somewhat empty areas it will be the exploitation of the country by those with the British sentiment. Above all this is the justice of the matter. All settlements set apart for colored people in a primitive condition of life, should have permanent water and all reservations should be unalienable under any circumstances.

4. Christian Missions

It is our considered opinion that emancipation and uplift can best be secured in co-operation with Christian Missions. This service is generally unselfish and certainly is most economical. We pay tribute to the work of all denominations among the aboriginal population.

5. Finance

We believe that all we ask for is financially possible in that we are sure that the work can be made self-supporting and any loans necessary would be self-liquidating. We affirm that justice supports our requests and the well being of the dark race demands that any scheme of uplift must be contributed to by the Dark race itself.

In presenting our wishes for your information we do genuinely appreciate your anxiety to do the best in the discharge of your trust and we extend to you our grateful thanks,

On behalf of the League, Yours sincerely

38. William Cooper, Secretary, Australian Aborigines' League, to the Editor, *Ladder*, 5 November 1936, *Ladder*, vol. 1, no. 4, June 1937

The white race, in its dealings with the dark race, seems always to think in terms that involve the aboriginal as something sub-human, or, at least, outcast. Many of our friends even seem to be infected with a superiority complex which is not fair to our race. May I plead for an attitude that will recognise our real humanity for, though we have suffered unspeakable horrors since the coming of the white race, we still have that self respect which causes a feeling of hurt when received with a superior and merely tolerant attitude.

My league very definitely appeals for a fair deal for the whole race, full blood or coloured. We definitely protest against discrimination in favour of any one section. Might I submit our claim in brief? The full-blood is the descendent of the race that has peopled this continent for many hundreds of years. The coming of the white race and the passing of the sovereignty should not have affected the title to his share of the soil, and his coming, by conquest, under British rule, should have brought him British citizenship with all the rights and privileges thereof. The attitude that only by virtue of some white blood can a native claim some consideration is definitely wrong. The aboriginal has a right to the best. The half-caste or preferably the coloured native, is descendent also of the aboriginal, and heir to all that such descendent involves. He is also son of the white man and I submit, heir to all that involves.

The supposed superiority of the half-caste is not admitted, and in fact, all thought of breeding the half-caste white, and the desire that that be accomplished, is a creature of the white mind. The coloured person has no feeling of repugnance toward the full blood, and in fact, he feels more in common with the full blood than with the white.

We dark folk have no regret that we are coloured, nor do we admit any fundamental superiority in being white. We are proud of our race. We know that a dark person, full blood or half-caste, can do anything he is shown how, and can do it as well as a white man. Our plea and aim is that the whole dark race be lifted to full modern culture, and be granted full equality in every way with the white race.

39. William Cooper, Secretary, Australian Aborigines' League, to the Premier, New South Wales, Bertram Stevens, 15 November 1936

There are two communications from my league to you which have not been acknowledged and one which received a somewhat evasive answer, or so it seemed to me. The dates of the communications were for the first two, February 19th. of this year, and of the latter May 16th. I am quite certain that the delay has been due to your overseas visit, and am just as sure that had the matters come to your notice in the normal way, you would have received them, and have given them your careful consideration. I am summarising the communications and request your earnest kindly consideration.

I requested that you hear a deputation from this league on some occasion when you are in Melbourne, as doubtless you will be from time to time. The requests are:

(1) That full citizen rights be accorded to all aborigines whether living on a settlement or not. This to include sustenance where aborigines are not able to secure work.

This league appeals for full rights as enjoyed by white people and naturalized aliens, these rights being civic, political and economic. We claim the right to work for full wages or the payment of full sustenance (dole) if unable to work. We contend that our women should receive the maternity bonus in cases of childbirth. In short, we claim the removal of all disabilities so that an aboriginal person shall have the same status as the white person, a maori or a naturalised alien. In our deputation we would seek to convince you of the capacity of every member of our race in N.S.W. for full citizenship.

(2) That no-one be expelled from an aboriginal station without an enquiry to be conducted by the A.P. Board and that the aboriginal charged in such cases be entitled to assistance (legal or otherwise).

We contend that many men and women have been expelled for no good reason as agitators. Some of these have been good christians of unblemished character. We do feel that some [expulsions], at least, have been irregular, being done by the manager without reference to the Board, or without the full case being presented. The cruel operation of expulsion is particularly felt when the person is old and desiring to go home in the evening of life. We appreciate the need of discipline, but this is aided when an inquiry takes place, as, if there should be any offence, due notice can be taken of it. The person will, if given a hearing, have the feeling of justice done. The assistance is asked for as one with a good case would be given the opportunity of presenting it satisfactorily.

(3) That lands occupied by aboriginals be developed by them, suitable instruction and necessary equipment being provided. When men are adequately trained, that opportunity be given to dark men to cultivate land for their own profit.

We will be able to show you that our men have been able to succeed in the past, and given a chance we are sure that many of them will succeed in the future. All we ask is that the lands now in use as aboriginal stations be fully exploited. When a native has proved his capacity for successful work, and capacity to manage his own affairs, he be allowed to settle land for his own profit. We are aware that reasons will be given to show the impracticability of this proposal, but we have a complete answer to any objectors. We feel that the native will be assured of some income, and that the costs of the A.P. Board will be reduced if a fair try out is given to this proposal. A definite preliminary proposal is set out at some length later in this letter.

(4) That the schools now provided for aboriginal children be raised to the standard of schools provided for white children and that the curriculum of native schools be the same as that in the schools of white children.

It is an open secret that dark children are not to receive education beyond the third grade and they are not getting it in the schools conducted by the department. We claim that our children should get the full opportunity of attaining the fullest primary education and for secondary education where the capacity is evident. Our people say that they want their children to be able to become doctors, nurses, teachers, etc., just as it has been possible for other natives, Fijian, Indian, etc., in other parts. We claim that our race is just as capable and you will appreciate that we only ask the chance of doing so where competence is present.

(5) That parliamentary representation be allowed to aboriginals in the same way as the maoris of New Zealand are catered for.

The maoris have four members in their legislature. Until the time that there is no aboriginal problem we do feel that a member in the House to present their case and conserve their interests is but fair.

In the matter of the development of aboriginal lands we submitted a proposal for a try out at Cumeroogunga, named because of its ideal situation on the Murray, with abundance of good water, with land easily irrigible, with fertility of soil and convenience to markets. We proposed as follows:

ORANGE CULTURE: At Madowla Park, near Cumeroogunga, there is a grove of trees from which an average of 1750 per year is obtained, giving employment to six men through the year, including aboriginals, by the way. We suggest a planting of a number of trees at Cumeroogunga. Of course other citrus fruits could be added according to the advice of your experts.

TOMATO CULTURE: This area would be quite as early as Echuca and the early crop would be marketable at profitable rates. The returns for the first year could cover all costs in connection with the planting. Late crops of the fruit could be pulped or distributed to the inhabitants of Cumeroogunga or other stations. There has been tomato culture at Cumeroogunga years ago, by certain of the dark folk. The breakdown of their pumping engine stopped what was a promising venture.

VINE CULTURE; TOBACCO CULTURE: Success is obtained in parallel circumstances elsewhere and we submit that experimental plots be established. We could add rice culture as the Murray flats can be so easily flooded for this cereal.

LUCERNE CULTURE: It is open to doubt if pig raising for the central markets would be a success, owing to the remoteness from the railhead at Picola (9 miles) and the distance from the markets. Ultimately curing would make it a possibility, but meantime an experimental plot of lucerne and a few cows and pigs would be of value, from the point of view of the instruction given and the supply of local needs.

FINANCE: We realise that this will be raised and in anticipation we would direct your attention to the Act of Congress, approved June 18th., 1934, to which you have doubtless access. (Public ... No. 383 ... 73rd. Congress). This Act provides for the development of Indian lands and for an appropriation from which loans could be made to Indians for the development of the lands. Our proposals could be made on a purely business basis, and we feel that there need not be any loss on the experiment. There will not be if the experiment be sympathetically made as a constructive move for the removal of admittedly difficult problems.

GOVERNMENT EXPERIMENTAL STATION: We suggested that the experimental work could be coupled with general experimental work as carried out by governments. This would enable your experts to couple with the ameliorative work for the aboriginals the matter of the exploitation of the Murray River lands, now so largely under forest, and yet of vast potential wealth. It may be that the dual aspect of our proposals will enhance the prospects of a thorough try out.

The labour for the work requiring to be done will be, of course, by the natives, who would work for sustenance received, receiving also a part of the profit according to the labour given.

Cumeroogunga is potentially wealthy. The people are very poor. We feel that such poverty in such potential wealth is wrong. We suggest that the needs of the people be related to the capacity of the soil for mutual advantage of the administration and the natives.

In submitting this I would be pleased if you would regard it as an earnest [demonstration] of the desire of the aboriginal to co-operate for his own uplift. I would suggest that our League can be, and is, willing to be of material aid in the uplift of our race. We therefore ask your most favourable consideration.

Yours sincerely

40. Australian Aborigines' League Annual Report, Year 1936

Dear Fellow Members of the Dark Race,

It is with mixed feelings that I report for the year. At times I get very discouraged at the slow progress of our cause and at other times the evidence of improvement heartens me. The fact is that there is continued improvement all the time of late years, but the rate of progress is too slow. At the moment, the Star of our Hope is in the ascendant. We have suffered enough, God knows, but surely the day of our deliverance is drawing nigh. I hope to live to see it. It is sad to think that all our miseries were uncalled for and that the intolerance of our position should be allowed to continue for a moment. It is wicked that a baptism of blood has been the portion of a people who have never given any provocation. Our friends among the white race are growing in numbers and interest, though we are often sorry to note that some of these regard us as inferior clay. We want equality. We are dark complexioned and we do not wish to be otherwise. It is not too much to ask for the recognition of our full humanity and the right of full uplift for every member of our race. Our work is a goodwill one. Any complaints we have to make we do make, and we do not compromise in respect of our just claims. We are most temperate in our submissions and we must say that, generally speaking, our correspondence is received with good spirit. With but little exception, the official and departmental attitude to us is considerate and we appreciate this and are pleased to set it on record.

The year has been a busy one. Every movement affecting our interests is watched carefully and due representations made when necessary. A programme of advance is kept before the authorities, and, as a result, correspondence is very heavy. Letters are received from every State and from England ...

41. William Cooper, Secretary, Australian Aborigines' League, to Sir John Harris, Secretary, Anti-Slavery and Aborigines Protection Society, 10 January 1937

Enclosed please find my comments, representing the opinion of our league in the matters referred to in yours of 25th Nov.

Your proposals are splendid and I trust you will be able to help us to secure what is our aim, viz: — the right to a share in our fatherland.

Comment on Statement drawn up by the Anti-Slavery and Aborigines Protection Society dated 25th November '36

We are thoroughly in agreement with the statement in respect of the Land Trust for Natives. Aboriginal administration and control is still dominated by the psychology of 100 to 150 years ago. It was then presumed that the aboriginal was little removed from the native fauna and legislated for accordingly. May I traverse some aspects of the matter.

As might have been expected, 100 to 150 years of contact with white civilisation has made a tremendous impact on native culture. Whole tribes have succumbed in the contact and in other cases only a meagre residue survived. This residue imbibed the culture of the white and has proved itself capable of doing anything the white can do. We have, as a result, native tradesmen (carpenters, etc) and natives trained in every phase of agricultural and pastoral industry. We have native clergy, teachers and even lady typists. In every field the native has proven himself most adaptable and we contend that "the native can do anything the white can do, if he is shown how". One of our half caste women is an A.L.C.M. (Associate of the London College of Music) and a daughter of this lady is one of the finest elocutionists I have heard. Still we are "aboriginals within the meaning of the act" which means we have no status in law. Certainly we enjoy some measure of liberty in certain parts but as a matter of Grace and not of Law. In some cases the possession of more than 50% of white blood gives us certain privileges; in other cases any aboriginal blood at all loses us the rights of the whites.

Maternity bonus
Aboriginal women are exempted by specific legislative determination from the bonus no matter how cultured. If a half caste woman is not receiving assistance from the Government she may get the bonus. If she is living in a Government reserve she is debarred. The white woman, the wife of a sustenance worker (on the dole as it is termed) gets the bonus, of course.

Sustenance — Dole
Excepting in Victoria, aboriginal men do not receive the dole. They may get rations but generally the able bodied men do not. They must get out and seek work which white men cannot get. Distress is rife as a result and T.B., resultant from under nourishment is all too common.

Old age and Invalid pensions
These are not available to any with more than half aboriginal blood. Others are supposed to get rations from the Government. I know of one case where a woman was refused a pension because she was more than half dark. When relief as an aboriginal was sought she was refused as she was more than half white. Such a contradictory position arises from the fact that pensions are disbursed by the Federal Authorities and aboriginal relief by the State.

Political Rights
These vary in the different States but most aboriginals have no rights.

All the above are available to Maoris or to aliens who have become naturalised.

Right to own land and to will it away on death
The aboriginal may not own anything as a right. If he acquires anything by his industry he has no right to will it and cases have occured where the Crown has taken over the property and sent the widow to a settlement as a pauper. Against all this we are in protest and it does appear that our outlook is definitely improving. Agitation will certainly bring us to our goal. Now to refer to the proposals in your statement: —

Reserves
This is a sore point. We have reserves set apart for natives. These are mainly on paper and if wanted by the white, as recently at Tennants Creek, in the

Northern Territory, the aboriginal is turned off and kept out. We contend that reserves should be inalienable and white entry should be only by authority. There should be a definite policy of development of such reserves by the natives for the natives with the end in view of their full uplift. We have reserves in some parts where the possibilities are limitless but the natives are idle and illnourished because wonderful lands are just under grass. (See the reference to Cumeroogunja in our Annual report for this year.)

Our men, trained in various pursuits connected with the land are clamouring for the right to a little of their fathers' lands that they may be able to earn an independency. We feel that this could be made a practicability by the advance of loans to approved trained natives. (See our programme as outlined in our Constitution sent you under separate cover.)

We note you[r] proposals in detail and these seem to be generally in accordance with our views. We do trust that you will, by your advocacy, be able to help us to full emancipation.

In passing we would emphasise the outstanding need, viz: — the Federalising of aboriginal control. The position is that those states with the largest aboriginal population has the smallest white population. Victoria can be generous for it has but a handful of natives to an enormous white population. Western Australia has a small white population but has 25% of Australia's aboriginals. It seems to be a matter of finance. The will to do better is present but the ability to do so is not. If the states with the largest population contributed on a per capita basis with the other States, the burden would be spread and a better deal be done by our race.

We feel, too, that we must get parliamentary representation. We want our advocate in parliament, seeking our rights and looking after our interests.

42. William Cooper, Secretary, Australian Aborigines' League, to the Prime Minister, Joseph Lyons, 16 January 1937

I take the liberty of enclosing for your information a copy of an agenda of suggestions for the forthcoming meeting of Chief Protectors of Aborigines and other administrative officers.

We looked forward to the late Premiers' conference as the means of our emancipation. Now that the consideration has been passed on to the administrative officers for consideration and recommendation we are hoping that our proposals will be kept in mind.

I will forward a copy also to the Minister for the Interior and one to each Minister of the Crown concerned and the Chief Protectors.

Our case is desperate in different parts and only by subsidy can the States hope to improve our lot. They have, in some cases, the will to do so but lack the financial capacity.

Yours sincerely

Australian Aborigines' League

AGENDA of proposals submitted by the Australian Aborigines' League for the consideration of the Conference of Chief Protectors and others.

1. That all aboriginal interests be federalised with a Federal Ministry for Aborigines. Failing this

2. That there be coordination between State Departments with a view to a common policy for the whole of the Commonwealth.

3. That a National Policy be formulated for the uniform and systematic uplift of the whole of the aboriginal population throughout Australia.

4. That the cost of administering the aboriginal policy be a charge, on a per capita basis, against the whole of Australia, thus enabling the States with a large white population and a comparatively small aboriginal population sharing [i.e. to share] the cost with States with a large aboriginal population and a relatively small white population.

5. That all approved aboriginals of full or part aboriginal blood be allowed to adopt an independent status and that, in that condition, they be not subject to any disabilities in law, political, civil or economic, as aboriginals. That such aboriginals be entitled to all the rights of white persons as maternity bonus, old age and invalid pensions, sustenance (work for dole and relief work) while unemployed, etc.

6. That all aboriginals of full or part blood have the right to live in reserves set apart for aboriginals. That expulsion from reserves for breach of discipline or other cause shall not be permitted without open enquiry at which the charged aboriginal shall be allowed assistance for his defence, legal assistance if desired. Any aboriginal discharged from an aboriginal station shall be treated in the matter of sustenance as an aboriginal electing to live privately, if unemployed.

7. That no advantage shall accrue to any class of aboriginal over another, i.e., that full bloods with those of any degree of mixed blood shall have equality of treatment and opportunity.

8. That the aboriginal population shall be grouped into classes determined by the stage of their progress and that the policy of the Administration shall be the progressive elevation from one class to an higher one till the whole race is fully civilised and cultured. These groups shall be:
    (a) Myall Aboriginals.
    (b) Partly civilised and detribalised aboriginals.
    (c) Civilised aboriginals.

9. That education be provided for all aboriginal children designed to permit all who are capable of qualifying, to attain to the highest standard. As may be justified, secondary schools for aboriginal children shall be provided. Where this is not possible, aboriginal children and young people shall have the right to attend secondary schools set apart for white children. The education of all aboriginal children shall be academic and vocational.

10. That all aboriginals be encouraged to work in the industry of civilisation; that they have the right to work and that all able-bodied unem-

ployed, aged, sick and infirm aboriginals shall have the assurance of full sustenance, the third group of aboriginals to be treated for sustenance as whites in parallel circumstances are treated, viz., payment of dole, old age or invalid pension, or as the case may be.

11. Suitable areas of land shall be set apart for the increasing aboriginal population. These should be large enough to permit of the development of full self-reliance, all community services being rendered, where possible, by aborigines. All reserves should be fully developed by the most up-to-date methods under expert direction. Young aboriginals should be encouraged to settle in these reservations but there should not be any compulsion on aged persons to leave areas that they have become attached to. Aboriginal reserves to be inalienable and whites not to be allowed thereon only by permission.

12. That trained and qualified aboriginals be allowed to settle on lands and to work them for their own profit, the ultimate design of all training in settlements being with this independency in view.

13. All offences by aboriginals to be subject to punishment only to the extent that white persons are punishable, due regard being paid to the implications of aboriginal law or psychology. Offences by whites against aboriginals to be punishable on the same basis as offences by whites against whites and offences by aboriginals to be punishable only to the same degree as in the case of offences by whites against whites. In other words there shall be full equality of whites and aboriginals before the law.

43. William Cooper, Secretary, Australian Aborigines' League, to Isaac Selby, 1 February 1937

With several other aboriginals I was present at Footscray on Sunday week when you, among others, gave an address at the anniversary of the landing of Batman. Some of us went with misgiving for what is a memorial of the coming of the Whites is a memorial of death to us. That Batman was kind and just to the aborigines is appreciated: that the coming of the whites spelt disaster to our forebears should also be borne in mind. Taking as an illustration, my tribe only. As a lad I can remember 500 men of my tribe, the Moiras, gathered on one occasion. Now my family is the only relic of the tribe. From being a populous people we have now only a remnant of several tribes, all desperately poor and suffering disabilities that are not put on the white race. We attended the meeting as a gesture to the chairman, Mr Claude Smith, a proven friend, but we were regaled with an address on the White Australia policy, no mention of the aborigines occurring.

I am writing to suggest that in future gatherings the notice of the white people be called to the presence of a residue, left after the white man satiated himself in the blood of the aboriginal, and that there should be a call for more than sympathy on their behalf. I know you will recognise the justice of our claim and feel that you will know just how to call attention to the wrong of perpetuating the crime of the days now happily gone, for though we may not suffer by shooting, poisoning or the like, the fact of our being debarred from the full rights of the white race still is censurable.

We were here before the whites and we claim that the coming of the whites should not involve our extermination or complete subjection. We claim that the day of restitution has come and that we should be accorded full equality of opportunity and responsibility with the whites. Those of our race who are as yet uncultured should be uplifted by a planned programme and no policy as the White Australia policy should regard the aboriginal as outside the scope of its benefits.

Thank you for your kindly references,

yours sincerely[59]

44. William Cooper, Secretary, Australian Aborigines' League, to the Minister for the Interior, Thomas Paterson, 18 February 1937

I am addressing you more personally than may be proper in departmental correspondence because I know that the concerns of my people are regarded by you as a personal responsibility as well as an official one. Because I know your heart is so genuinely in the matter I am writing again when perhaps it may be thought that I am over anxious and importunate.

I am sure you will understand that the Aboriginal problems have a different reaction to we civilised aboriginals than even to the most kindly disposed white persons, unless it be to the very small number who have learned to "think black". Generally the average kindly disposed white person is willing to wait the outworking of an ameliorative scheme but we continue to suffer meanwhile.

I am chiefly concerned about two aspects both of which are under the consideration of your department and both of which I know will be handled by you in a Statesmanlike and Humanitarian way. Of this I am convinced and thoroughly appreciative but — and you will not consider my importunity unreasonable — we continue to suffer while the remedy is not applied. Naturally we want our suffering minimised first and ended as soon as possible though we realise that the implementing of your policy is going to be difficult, because white Australia, however kindly disposed, does not, cannot, "think black". We are merely something inferior, biological specimens, anthropological exhibits, rather than weaker brothers. This I say without passion for the psychology of the native is not retributive or vengeful. We do feel that if we had manifested these attributes, while we may have suffered more at the time, our militancy would have won a standing for us comparable with the Maoris. We merely plead as an inconsequential minority for kindliness of heart on the part of our white brothers that will lead them to plan our uplift and culture to the full European standard. The fact that some of us have been civilised, not by any plan but despite its absence, is proof of what can come with a plan carefully considered and patiently applied. Do you know that I feel that a definite plan of uplift, which we could apply ourselves if we had the financial capacity would raise the present generation so far from the present primitive conditions that they would scarcely be recognized as the same people but our hope is the rising generation. We desire to help the present generation as much as possible but the child now and to be should be the chief concern. These, coming into civilised conditions would be quite civilised by the time they reached adult age. We further believe that their civilisation will not provoke any new problem but will lead to the removal of the present ones in due course. In the aboriginal you have all the man power required for the development of Australia's unsettled parts if they are given due training, direction and leadership and, might I add, inspiration, and its peopling by a population not merely European in culture but British in sentiment and loyalty would be a bulwark of defence. You are yet to find that the aboriginal race of Australia will be as worthy as any other colored race in the empire, units making for the stability of Australia and the defence of our heritage. All this is in the power of the white community and its administrative arm, but neglect of this cannot be otherwise than serious.

My reason in writing is, firstly, to say that I am disappointed in not hearing anything further as to the implementing of the announced policy now some months old. This did not concern us so greatly when we understood that a conference of aboriginal administrators was to be held this month (February) but its postponement perturbed us. If we even knew that further consideration of your policy was pending the conference we would have been contented but we do not know if there is any relation of the one to the other. Would you kindly make a pronouncement as to the implementing of the announced policy.

The second reason for writing, of far less general import than the one mentioned because it springs from the conditions obligating that policy, is yet of the more pressing import at the moment. It is the matter of the sale of the lubras to the Japanese. It is easy to think and to say that "the men are only too willing to sell the girls" and to white psychology this seems to be correct. It is fundamentally incorrect. In the clash of culture the white person is apt to get the wrong perspective on the aboriginal mind. We are opposed to wrongdoing and, under our laws, our fathers killed any base characters on the principle that if they were dead they could not propagate their kind. The clash of cultures made practices, not unwholesome in the aboriginal setting, extremely unwholesome by distortion and exploitation. Economic causes are the root of the trouble on Bathurst Island and elsewhere. Shortage of food is the basic cause of the sale of the women.

Mr Paterson, my distress is that my people are suffering and the remedy is wholly in your hands. Our girls are taken on to vessels there to be the vehicles of Asiatic lust. These girls are used as long as they can be and are then thrown overboard. Any who get back to their people only do so to corrupt them the more with acquired disease and to live a life of misery themselves. Generally they will not get ashore and it were better so.

The law is there — it is broken — and we suffer, and while suffering is the portion of the aboriginal, the cry of the people goes up to a God of deliverance. You are the only Moses who can lead the sufferers into the Promised Land.

That these are my people gives me the right to ask for adequate patrol of the coast but, more than that even, for the assured sustenance for the natives, including meat (goat flesh is most suitable) to be made available through the Mission on the Island.

Thanking you for all you have done ...

45. William Cooper, Secretary, Australian Aborigines' League, to Sir John Harris, Secretary, Anti-Slavery and Aborigines Protection Society, 16 March 1937

Steady improvement in prospects, if not yet in actual experience, characterises the administration of Mr Lyons as Prime Minister of Australia, as far as aboriginal matters are concerned and we are glad to pay this tribute. Still we have to plead our cause and argue our rights and in one matter in particular we are seeking your assistance. It may be that the changing battleground gives us advantages and when Mr Lyons arrives in London it will be to our advantage to impress on him that his responsibilities follow him.

I am forwarding herewith a copy of our correspondence with the Prime Ministers Dept. which gets nowhere with the usual departmental disposition to introduce red herrings or evade the point at issue. You are familiar with every aspect of the case, I know, but you will permit me to reiterate. We claim the right to advance to full European culture and we feel that the time is "ripe and rotten ripe" for a plan to take the place of the haphazard of the past. The aborigines must no longer be regarded as a necessary evil but a responsibility. We are the potential solution of the neglected empty spaces and a plan of culture, giving the aboriginal the status of manhood, will result in the peopling of the vast hinterland so unsuited to the European, with a virile race capable of developing the vast resources of Australia. A statesmanlike policy will make Australia safe to the Empire for the Aboriginal is more British often than the white. They are intensely loyal to the person of the King and the Empire and as they lose the primitive culture, destined to ultimately perish, they assume the culture of Britain. Trained in modern conditions, the aboriginal will be the bulwark of the defence system as it affects the country so peculiarly his own. How preferable is this policy for settling Australia to bringing in of Southern Europeans, a policy which is already disadvantageous where it has been done.

In the matter particularly in question at the moment we would refer you to the letter of Mons. Gsell. In this respect we ask your support of our claims and the endeavour, as may be possible, to secure the agreement of Mr Lyons to the request for additional support for missions in respect of the work that is peculiarly the responsibility of the Government and not the missions, viz: — sustenance and education.

Appreciating greatly the work you are doing for us,

I remain,

yours sincerely

46. William Cooper, Secretary, Australian Aborigines' League, to Isaac Selby, 16 March 1937

The kindliness of your references to our people at the Batman memorial, to which I have referred previously, and your sympathetic gesture in sending my letter to the "Herald" has shown me how genuinely you are our friend and it is a pleasure to count you in with the noble army who agree that when we ask for "A fair deal for the dark race" we are not asking anything unreasonable ... I am writing now to tell you of the result of your sending the letter for publication.

First I should like to say that I have not had good success in getting publicity and many letters sent have apparently reached only the Editors' wastepaper baskets. I have at times been very grieved at the refusal to publish for my letters are always marked with moderation, an aboriginal characteristic, if I may be permitted to mention something well known, and for their avoidance of anything which may be thought offensive. I have always felt that the path for me to take is that of winning by the sheer justice of our cause, though believe me, aboriginal folk do feel the indignities put on them and many a camp fire has heard the old folk tell the younger ones of the baptism of blood that has been our portion. But to tell you of the result of your letter: —

I had not expected publicity and when one after another referred to my letter in the "Herald" I was at a loss to follow what it was all about. When I received letters, including one from a Collins Street specialist, who is, out of hours, interested in the cause of the right, inviting me to meet him to talk over the matter, you can see the letter has caused a stir. Papers have referred to it with suitable comment, and altogether, you have been able to do more for us that we would have been able to do ourselve[s.] For this, very many thanks.

With sincere greetings

47. William Cooper, Secretary, Australian Aborigines' League, to the Premier, New South Wales, Bertram Stevens, 31 March 1937

I have written from time to time asking for the favor of your receiving a deputation from us when you are in Melbourne and I would be grateful if you would personally agree to see us at some convenient time: meantime I am asking your personal consideration of one outstanding matter as follows: —

As you may know, Cumeroogunja is located on the Murray, where an abundant supply of beautiful water exists. There is a pumping plant and water is laid on to some of the homes. The land is fertile and it must be patent that if the natives were encouraged to grow vegetables their health would be better. We are criticised for not doing so but the fault is not ours.

During the heat of the summer, a member of our executive noticed the dark folk passing to and from the stream with kero tins, drawing water from the river. He questioned the matter with the Assistant Manager who did then pump twice a day when he was there. When he went away one filling was reverted to per day and again, in the heat of the summer, the natives had to cart water by bucket. Now, only a matter of oil fuel stands between an adequate supply of water laid on and the conditions which did exist. I am at a loss to understand why two or even three pumpings per day cannot be made. It may be urged that the natives would waste the water. Would you accept that excuse from white people in similar circumstances? See that the taps are capable of being turned off, ration the use of water for gardens so that different people can use it at different times, forbid wasting and follow up disregard and there could not be any trouble on that score. There are other matters that I have put to you concerning the station which cost may have been a factor in not according to, but the cost of adequate water would be very low.

Can we have the assurance that next summer will see adequate water. If so, we can use our voice to bring to the notice of the people that we have secured this advantage and they must help us to retain it.

The present manager, who we hold in high regard [J. G. Danvers], will be able to warn any defaulter of the consequences of disregard of instructions and, if to this be added the weight of native opinion, I do not anticipate any difficulty whatever.

Thank you, Yours sincerely

48. William Cooper, Secretary, Australian Aborigines' League, to the Premier, New South Wales, Bertram Stevens, 9 May 1937

I do thank you for your letter of 24th ult. and for the promise of improved water supply at Cumeroogunja. This will make possible the further improvements I have advocated on behalf of our League. I am writing because that matter is not mentioned nor did you promise the deputation sought.

Aboriginal interests have been subordinated to financial considerations but I note by the press that the N.S.W. budget is now balanced so that our interests may be able to receive more notice. Will you please do this?

I would, however, point out that all we seek is the right to prove our capacity for self support. We have the water and the climate. The markets are available and surely we natives are entitled to a share of these markets with Chinese and other aliens.

Some years ago the natives of Cumeroogunja had a small pump with which they irrigated a small patch of tomatoes. The break down of that plant put an end to that small industry. Could not a start be made with tomatoes this year. The manager could oversee the work and the natives do it, the proceeds being distributed among the workers in relation to the labor put in. We are merely asking for a chance to prove that aboriginal control and uplift can be made a self-supporting matter. It can, therefore, be made a means of training for self-reliance and independence.

Might I request that you call for our correspondence and refer it to your agricultural department for investigation and I would be glad to hear further from you; also please consider the request for a deputation when we can answer your objections as well as explain our wishes.

Can we not ask that the 150th anniversary of your State have as one of its objectives the Honest endeavour to lift the aboriginal to the right to full manhood and British citizenship.

Yours sincerely

49. The Aboriginal Choir (leaflet)

THE ABORIGINAL CHOIR

The Aborigines will give the programme at the Celebration of the 102nd Anniversary of Melbourne's Birthday : : English and Aboriginal Songs

IN THE AUSTRALIAN CHURCH, RUSSELL STREET

MONDAY EVENING, 31ST MAY, 1937

- Cummeragungee Chimes
- Duets and Quartets
- A Harp and Gum Leaf Orchestra
- Playing on Hoop Iron
- All Things turned to Melody, as in Bush Land
- Six Little Native Girls
- The Laughing Nigger
- The Lyre Bird

IN AID OF THE OLD PIONEERS' MEMORIAL FUND

DR JAMES BOOTH Presides

Lecturette by ISAAC SELBY

Doors open at 7.15

Orchestra at 8 o'clock

Body of Church 1/- [Front Seats 2/-]

50. William Cooper, Secretary, Australian Aborigines' League, to the Minister for the Interior, Thomas Paterson, 16 June 1937

I am addressing you personally for the matters I have to communicate are so important from the Aboriginals' point of view that we wish to know that the matters have your own personal consideration.

You may have heard that I have a petition to the King signed by some 2000 members of my race, setting out our disabilities and praying the intervention of His Majesty to intervene for the prevention of the further extinction of our race and that we be granted representation in the Federal Parliament.

This petition was ready for despatch some two years ago and I had already consulted the Military Secretary to the Governor-General as to its presentation to His Excellency for Despatch to his Majesty when the promise was made that the future of our race would be considered at the next meeting of the Premiers, to be held in August 1936. Because we felt that there was a generally improved attitude toward the former owners of the land and in view of the definitely sympathetic attitude of the Hon. The Prime Minister and yourself we held over the presentation of the petition till this meeting could consider the matter. This meeting proved abortive, as far as the aboriginal cause was concerned, consideration being deferred to a meeting of departmental officers to be held in February 1937. This meeting was postponed till April and though it was held then, the only announcements in the press are the usual matters, which, coming from the Administration whose reaction to the aboriginal problem we find objectionable, is all we could expect. We feel that all the delay, all the expense, all the talk is just to result in "As you were". We looked to the political field, representative of public opinion, and we were shuffled on to the Administration, which has never been sympathetic, but always repressive.

Frankly, I am disappointed. We did look to this move as marking an epoch in our history. We asked [for] bread. We scarcely seem likely to get a stone. We are not surprised that the Administration gave scant notice, in the lack of expressed public opinion, to organisations of white people, who are not sufferers, but we did expect that when the native voice was organised to speak for itself, being actual sufferers, some notice would be taken.

Imposed on, defrauded, exploited, oppressed, we have no redress because our oppressors are private people but when it is a matter of administration we feel that we can claim British justice, which should remedy our wrongs without further delay.

I am aware that the old bogey of Finance will be urged but with the passing of the depression every other class of the community demands and gets relief. The greatest sufferers should be the first relieved but we claim "*THAT ABORIGINAL UPLIFT CAN, AND SHOULD BE MADE SELF-LIQUIDATING*".

For five long years our league has been functioning and seeking the removal of the 150 years old oppression. We have got nothing definite except the refusal of our claim for representation in the Federal Parliament — no result but a refusal — and no prospects but continued exploitation. 80,000 aborigines in Australia deliberately kept from uplift and refused one representative in Parliament. Yet in New Zealand the same number of natives have four members and one minister for Native Affairs. Our need is greater because our people are scattered. We only ask for a member with the same status as the Member for the White Population in the Territories. We quote this separate representation as a precedent but urge our much larger numbers as a better reason for representation than has the white population of the Territories.

We did the reasonable thing in withholding our petition to his Majesty for two long years, but unless we are assured that something definite will be done without further delay we will go ahead and solicit the intervention of His Majesty, which we believe we have the right to do and which prerogative the King has the right to exercise.

The aboriginal is poor, desperately poor, and designedly kept poor and no white man of means is sufficiently interested in our cause to spare of his means something for our uplift. If we had the means ourselves, or if it was made available we are sure that the first expense would be the greatest and that progress would be possible by the profits of the venture. We claim that the native has a right to live in the "Land of His Fathers". We claim he has the right to this without the need for working for it but we know that this is not desirable and would do harm to the race. We therefore claim the right to work for our living under modern conditions. We want the right to full education, academic, cultural and industrial and to be able to take our place beside the white race in full equality and responsibility. We ask the right to be fully British. In claiming this we protest with all our might against the discrimination between the full blood and the half caste. All are aboriginals and prefer to be so. Even near whites are more disposed to lean to the aboriginal side of the ancestry than the white.

The whole attitude of the administration is framed without regard to native opinion and from the assumption that the dark man admits the superiority of the White and desires incorporation in that race. This is most decidedly wrong.

The two races, side by side yet distinct, cannot be with any prejudice to the white race for our numbers are so inconsequential beside the number of whites. Equality in law will not mean actual equality as we know we must still suffer the disability of a minority and of color but equality in law is what we are asking.

Given time you will find that the dark race will prove an asset to Australia, being British to the core and loyal to a man.

While I have necessarily had to speak candidly, you will know that it is not personal. We know how well meaning the Prime Minister and yourself are and this we appreciate. We are further withholding the petition for a little longer while we ask what is the utmost you are prepared to do in the way of remedying our injustices.

With best wishes,
On behalf of the League,
Yours sincerely

51. William Cooper, Secretary, Australian Aborigines' League, to the Minister for the Interior, Thomas Paterson, 25 June 1937

I do thank you for your willingness to discuss the matter of the aborigines with me by letter. It is but another token of your genuine desire to do the right by my people. You say my previous letter was in a pessimistic strain. Mr Paterson, I am an old man and I did hope to live to see my people in a fair way to uplift. My hopes are not being realised, hence my despair. If my claims for my people are just, why should I not look for immediate relief. If they are unreasonable cannot I claim to be shown in what way they are. I am being assured all round that what we ask is only our right and therefore I feel that I am right when I persistently press for this right.

I am delighted at the assurance that your colleagues in the Federal Cabinet are likeminded with you and the Prime Minister in sincere desire to do the very best by our people.

I understand that the Federal Parliament has jurisdiction only over such aborigines as may live in the Territories. There are over 18,000 full bloods in these parts and I venture the opinion that if the Federal Government deals adequately with the problem as it affects the aborigines under its control a definite lead will be given to the State Governments and a favorable psychology will be developed in the general public.

Mr Paterson, your kindness is so genuine that I feel I can respectfully say to you, without impropriety, that you should, just for the moment, forget that you are a white man so that you may look at the matter as we do. To see things as we do, to feel as we do, is the best way to realise the extent of our disabilities. We do not want our people to remain primitive, uncultured and a prey to all comers. Why should we remain in the near Stone Age? The British were once where we are now. The conquering power of Rome, whatever else it did, lifted the British to culture and civilisation. We want that same uplift. Are we unreasonable?

We have proven our capacity, all over Australia, to become capable in every form of husbandry. In places we have made ourselves indispensable. We have acquired the faculty for the arts and crafts of civilisation, our men drive motor cars, are expert motor mechanics and engineers. We have orators, ordained clergymen, teachers and singers and I venture to say that our people, so capable of imitation, are to be found in every phase of modern culture. ALL WE HAVE ATTAINED TO HAS BEEN MERELY PICKED UP. WHAT WE WOULD HAVE BEEN WITH PLANNED UPLIFT MAY ONLY BE ASSUMED. We want our yet uncultured brothers to get the uplift we have received but we claim it should come by plan. Our uplift came throughout by a baptism of blood and only to a residue, the rest being destroyed by the contact. We are asking that, on their own reservations, according to the capacity of the soil, the dark people be trained in modern methods of agriculture. Progress will not be meteoric but we feel that it can be made practically self-liquidating. We urge that this should be the aim and the plan can be tried out experimentally first.

While not presuming more than to make a suggestion, we feel that planned uplift can be made through Christian missions more cheaply. We submit that the Commonwealth should supply the requisite machinery and expert supervision or advice. Whether the work is carried out by the departmental officers or by missionaries, under Government supervision, the uplift should be associated with educational facilities for the children, which should be progressively raised in status until the aboriginal child has the same educational facilities as the white child.

Now, still looking at our problems from the point of view of the native, please forget the white man's discrimination between the half caste and the full blood. Except where the notion is put into the head of the half caste no one thinks of the white strain at all. All are aborigines and content to be so, proud to be so. The full blood is a full man and fully British and fully entitled to uplift. Our only thought in respect of preference to half-castes is pleasure that someone is getting something and the more the better.

There is nothing fantastic in our claim for full uplift for the aboriginal. To settle the matter as we suggest will confer a twofold benefit: — It will settle the problem of the aboriginal and settle it justly.

Now as to why we want a Parliamentary representative in the Federal House. Nearly 20,000 aborigines, including half castes, are surely not asking too much when they request what a handful of whites in the Territories have now got. We feel that a member representing our race can maintain contact with our people, study their needs and present their claims. He can watch legislation with a view to seeing that his constituency is not omitted or penalised. He can initiate legislation. Though he would have no voice in respect of other states, he would have members privileges when travelling and his opinion might be of value as an interpretation of aboriginal thought. AND, THE ABORIGINAL WOULD ONLY HAVE WHAT THE MAORI NOW HAS AND WHAT THE GOVERNMENT OF SOUTH AFRICA IS PROPOSING FOR THE NATIVES THERE.

Mr Paterson, We claim that, given a trial, we will prove that we are capable of producing a yeomanry that can open up and develop the outback better than anyone else. We are acclimatised, and as our primitive people become civilized, they lose the aboriginal culture and outlook taking on the psychology of the white man. The aboriginal is loyal to the Throne and Person of this Majesty. The development of Australia by civilized aborigines is therefore sound in that it provides a bulwark for the defence of your land and ours.

I do hope that the administration of which you are so Honored a member will have the privilege of initiating the movement for emancipation of my people, in which you will have our full co-operation of my people, and that we will have an earnest of your good will by an early installment of reform is the earnest prayer of

Yours sincerely

52. Extract from William Cooper to Secretary, Australian Aborigines Amelioration Association [c. July 1937], *Ladder*, vol. 1, no. 5, October 1937

We are getting on quite nicely. The reaction of authority, at first suspicious, is now quite cordial and we feel that good is being done. Especially am I pleased with the reaction of Mr Paterson and Mr Lyons, in the order given. Certainly we have not yet got past the promise stage but our representations have led to definite promise which we hope will materialise. We know the biggest hurdle will be the entrenched departmental officials, to whom we are but clay (and this applies to your State, as well as to other States and the Commonwealth). Even in New South Wales we have had encouraging replies, though only after long ignoring and later evasion. At our instance, Cumeroogunja, on the wonderful Murray, is to be supplied with an up-to-date and powerful pumping plant and water is to be laid on to new homes which are to be built. The last thing we were able to secure was the provision of an area of land to be fenced and worked as a market garden. We asked for the culture of tomatoes, vines, oranges, lucerne, tobacco, etc., all possible in our fertile area, so well watered by the Murray. Only official apathy can prevent our request for a model aboriginal station to prove the inmates, and ultimately to be a pattern for Commonwealth-wide imitation, from being a success. Our petition for the King has been ready for dispatch for some time. We held it up to see what the last Premiers' Conference would bring forth. We further held it up to see what the conference of Chief Protectors would do. When this proved abortive, as far as we are concerned, we notified Mr Lyons that we had the petition ready for dispatch and the next move is with the Government. If it satisfies us we will not forward the petition ...

53. *Herald*, 7 August 1937, Clive Turnbull, 'Aborigines Petition the King'

Australia has never given her native people a fair deal. In this interview, Mr W. Cooper, spokesman of the aborigines and secretary of the Aborigines' League, pleads for opportunity, by education and general help, for the aborigine to become a citizen fit to take his place in the forefront of Australian life.

"Why should not the aborigines themselves develop the north?" he asks. And, but for the iniquitous treatment which for the last century they have received, he sees no reason why we should not already have had aboriginal doctors, lawyers and airmen.

Mr Cooper is 76 and hopes to see a change for the better before he dies. He is doing all he can to bring it about. Like many of his countrymen, he is a fluent talker.

He had but seven months' regular schooling when he was a youth. Much of his childhood he spent in the household of Sir John O'Shanassay, in Camberwell, and his young manhood he spent on pastoral properties.

More than 60 years ago he saw the remains of the Burke and Wills Expedition at Cooper's Creek.

I went to talk to him because I have long been interested in the problem of the aborigines. My own countrymen in Tasmania by a combination of cruelty and stupidity, succeeded in exterminating a whole race within 75 years.

The Victorian aborigines are going the same way…

"Education and opportunity will overcome the problems of the aborigine," he said.

"Our aims are set forth in the constitution of the Australian Aborigines' League. The immediate programme of the league is the progressive education of the aboriginal race by education and training in the arts and crafts of European culture.

"For primitive aborigines, while they remain primitive, we ask [for] the unalienable possession of adequate reserves to which white men shall have access only by authority from the Chief Protector.

"We ask that offences by white men against aborigines shall be punished by similar penalties to those for similar offences against white men, and to ask for special courts recognising tribal laws. We ask for education and industrial training.

"For the semi-civilised and detribalised natives we ask for reserves of agricultural land, the right to work and provision of full rations when no work is available, full rations to aged and infirm natives, and free education in State schools or in special schools.

"For civilised natives we ask the provision of agricultural land machinery, the right to work, invalid or old-age pensions, and complete educational and political rights.

"We are human. We may be uneducated by white standards: we are fully educated by our own. I do not know whether all colored peoples are the same, but we have a very high moral code and the principles of Christianity are part of our life.

"We want to get up to the same standards as the whites. But we are coming to the end of our tether. Now we are sending a petition to the King".

MR COOPER took down a great roll of signatures. "If we cannot get full justice in Australia we must ask the King", he said. "Some tell us that the King has no power now in these things, but we shall try anyway. There are 2000 signatures here, from aborigines all over Australia, not only in the towns, but at Palm Island, Bathurst Island and other distant places. Those who could not sign their own names have made their marks".

... "Up till the present time the condition of the aborigines has been deplorable", Mr Cooper said. "Their treatment was beyond human reason until the Lyons Government came in. I speak of a man as I find him, and I find Mr Lyons a gentleman. His Government is the first in the history of Australia to take up the cause of the aborigines. But it is not enough.

"Before that things were bad indeed. I am very very sorry that the white people of Australia must carry the bloodstains of the aborigines for evermore. It was the doing of uneducated white people and criminals in the first place, and the tradition of cruelty was handed down from white generation to generation to the present day.

"Fortunately the present generation of white people is becoming more sympathetic. That is very encouraging to me. I sit here working hour after hour in correspondence with my people thinking. How can we save them?

"I feel for my people as anyone would. Now the shootings, poisonings, and extermination have ceased, so far as I can tell. I get letters from Palm Island, from Mount Isa, from Central Australia, and all parts of Australia from my countrymen, and there is a great improvement in their treatment. We must give the present Government credit for that.

"But for our principal needs, what is done? We talk to politicians, and they say, Yes, they'll do this, and do that, but the years go on, and what is done?

"We need education, and we need industry. You will never bring our people forward without those things. The policy of the Governments at present will keep them laborers all their lives. You may read the views even of sympathetic white men. But they are not our views. We are the sufferers; the white men are the aggressors.

"We need a modern technical school for our people. You may ask where is the money to come from. But we have lost countless millions to the whites — the whole wealth of Australia. Are we not entitled to this? Must we lose our money as well as our lives?

"Our people should be given the training so that they may become doctors and nurses and teachers and teach our tribes the rules of hygiene and the best ways of living. But instead of lifting our people up, the early comers to our country destroyed them.

"They were destroying people better than themselves! If we had been a treacherous race they might have been excused. But there is no excuse for the murders which were committed upon us. There is no excuse for taking a man's life away without cause.

"Yet if these people had been different, how different already might have been our story! Then you would have had already a colored race that Australia could be proud of. We should have been soldiers, doctors, airmen. We have the courage and the resource.

"Now our people have nothing: all was taken from them. They will never have anything so long as the present state of things endures. They will be laborers, rabbit-trappers, casual fishermen perhaps.

"Nor do I think you can ever bring the present generation of aborigines up to the highest standard. They have a horror and fear of extermination. It is in the blood, the racial memory, which recalls the terrible things done to them in years gone by.

"Even now they do not like to say much. They think, 'If we open our mouths we will lose even what little we have'. But the next generation of aborigines: you can bring them up to any standard you like.

"In Fiji, not very long ago, the people were cannibals. Now they have their own doctors and lawyers and professional men. Is it not shameful that Australia should be so backward in training her native people?

"Now we hear much of developing the north. Why should not our own people develop it? Why will the Government not let us have a chance to do it, to make our own State in our own country?"

54. William Cooper, Secretary, Australian Aborigines' League, to the Prime Minister, Joseph Lyons, 26 October 1937

Thank you for your acknowledgement of our petition to His Majesty and the promise of fullest sympathy and consideration. We know you will give this and we do thank you for the definite interest you have in our cause. I would, however, offer the following comment in respect of the penultimate clause of letter of the 17th inst. and would request that these comments be in mind in the consideration promised.

His Majesty is King of Australia, and on this account, the State control of aborigines should not prevent consideration being given on a national basis. I am not, therefore, able to appreciate the reference to the natives of the

Territory in particular and to the jurisdiction of the State Governments. We do trust that the division of the administration over State Legislatures, which is always to our detriment, will not retard our relief. With all respect, since our petition is to the King of Australia, it should not be possible for divided control hurting us in this instance.

Respecting the conference of Chief Protectors, from which we scarcely expected relief, and which so far as we can see only resulted in one decision which was not previously operative, and that the recognition of the wives of aboriginals married according to Tribal Law being recognised as legal wives and thus not being compellable witnesses. From our point of view the conference was only a waste of time. We did expect a Magna Carta from the Premiers' Conference but from the conference of Chief Protectors we only got the confirmation of our humiliation. Frankly, we are alarmed at the intention to seek advice from countries where Negro populations constitute the dark problem, for we, not withstanding all our indignity, are allowed to walk on footpaths, ride in public vehicles and trains and put up in many hotels where white men are residing. To add to our sorrows the humiliation of our dark brethren in the curfew and the pass system would be degradation indeed. In due course we will present you with our comment on the published minutes of the conference but meantime we are in protest against the whole result. We do claim that the forwarding of our petition be not clouded with the State aspect or the atmosphere of the Chief Protectors' conference.

Respecting our claim for parliamentary representation, we very definitely submit that the Maori population is approximately the same as our people, with any advantage to us. In an area the size of Victoria they have four members and a Ministry for Native Affairs, which has had a native minister. We are persisting in our claim for one who can speak for us in Parliament, influencing legislation on our behalf and safeguarding us from administrational officers who, with notable exceptions, interpret their responsibilities to the aborigines in much the same way as a gaol governor does his criminal population. Our desire is a change of heart in the electorate, reflected in Parliament and leading to a policy which will be different from that administered by our gaolers. So far from divided control being allowed to retard our securing representation, we feel that our member should have the right to sit in every legislature, and any constitutional difficulty could be overcome by legislation. If our member were a member of the Senate, perhaps as this is the States' Rights House, any difficulty might be more easily overcome.

Hoping to hear shortly of the granting of our requests.

I remain, etc.

55. *Argus*, 26 October 1937, 'Petition to the King: Grievances of Aborigines'

For the first time in history Australian aborigines have petitioned the King. The document prepared by Mr W. Cooper, honorary secretary of the Australian Aborigines' League, asks that the race be protected by granting it the power to propose a member of the Federal Parliament as its representative.

The petition has been signed by 1,814 aborigines from all parts of Australia, mostly from mission stations. It has been sent to the Governor-General for despatch to the King by the hands of the Prime Minister, who has already acknowledged receipt of the petition and promised to give it early consideration.

The text of the petition runs ...

56. *Argus*, 13 November 1937, 'Aborigines' Day of Mourning: Plan for 150th Anniversary'

Plans for the observance by aborigines throughout Australia of a "day of mourning" simultaneously with the 150th anniversary celebrations in Sydney, were announced at a meeting last night convened by the Australian Aborigines' League.

"While white men are throwing their hats into the air with joy", said the chairman (Mr A. P. A. Burdeu), "aborigines will be in mourning for all that they have lost."

It was hoped, Mr Burdeu added, that the day of mourning would direct the attention of the people of Australia to the desire of the aborigines for full rights of citizenship.

Stating that he was proud of his aboriginal blood, Mr William Ferguson, organising secretary of the Aborigines' Progressive Association of New South Wales, said that aborigines did not want protection. "We have been 'protected' for 150 years, and look what has become of us", he said.

"Scientists have studied us and written books about us as though we were some strange curiosity, but they have not prevented us from contracting tuberculosis and other diseases which have wiped us out in thousands".

Mr Ferguson complained bitterly of the treatment of aborigines at aboriginal settlements in New South Wales. "It would be better for the authorities to turn a machine-gun on us", he said.

Mr Douglas Nicholls, a leading Fitzroy footballer, who is an aborigine, said that aborigines were not satisfied merely to be kept alive by a weekly issue of rations. "We do not want chicken food", he said. "We are not chickens; we are eagles".

Resolutions were passed urging the development of North Australia by aborigines in preference to non-British Europeans.

57. William Cooper, Secretary, Australian Aborigines' League, to Sir John Harris, Secretary, Anti-Slavery and Aborigines Protection Society, 22 December 1937

In your article on "The Tragedy and Romance of the Australian Natives" of October 1937, there is a certain element of optimism which is bound to mislead those who are not in the position to know the true state of affairs. TRAGEDY, yes, a thousand times more than has ever been told, but ROMANCE, no, not for my people, not since the white man has set foot on our shores.

You say that "a remarkable change has taken place in the attitude of Australian Public Opinion and the Australian Governments toward the aboriginal inhabitants of the continent". "It would be difficult", you further state, "to find another instance of such a rapid rise of a primitive people, from a position of inferiority, neglect and contempt to one of real national concern".

No one more than myself could desire so ardently that things were as you think they are. How I wish it were as you say. Then, the pretty picture which adorns the front page of your paper would be justified and true.

How glad and grateful my people are for the few white friends who, like you, Dear Sir John, are genuinely interested in our cause and who are actually working on our behalf, I cannot find words to tell. But, as regards the Public, as a whole, even here at Home, so to say, in Australia, there is ignorance, indifference, and even the same old superiority complex of the white man toward the colored — for, as you must know, the White Australia policy excludes us, the aborigines of this continent.

This "striking change", you continue, has been effected chiefly because, at long last, the real merits and capacities of the aborigines has been brought home to the knowledge and conscience of the Australian people". Alas, this is not so. With very few exceptions, the white people here have neither the knowledge nor the conscience which you have in mind. On the contrary, our friends among the white Australians and our own educated aborigines, all agree that the prevalent attitude among those who at all take an interest in us is that the blackfellow is a "low, almost sub human creature, and the sooner he dies out the better". And this is shown in practice by the way in which the blackman is treated: killing of aboriginals by constables and other white men is still a very frequent occurance: the taking away of hunting grounds and replacing the people by bullocks to fatten on these grounds, thus forcing the aboriginals to die in the barren desert, is still practiced: the disgraceful and shameful treatment of our girls by the white men is still as prevalent as ever, and even our rulers seem to support such behaviour, as it appears, for instance, from such parliamentary debates as reported in Hansard No. 11 of last year in Western Australia and the material conditions of life on Government Mission stations are such as no white man would tolerate for his own people, aside from the indignity of segregation.

Our Prime Minister tells us that he and his cabinet are much concerned about the aboriginals, but the problem is to know how exactly to help us. Surely that is no problem, for it is plain that we need food, shelter, education, civilisation, and, finally, complete emancipation. We do not want policemen to rule over us and cattlemen to "civilise" us. We need and want the cooperation of the educated, kindly and sympathetic white people, backed by the financial power of the Federal Government, to bring education, culture and industry to my people so that we may become partners in the work of our country — the Commonwealth of Australia. And I maintain that my people have the ability, the intelligence and the unspoiled native power, if given the opportunity and the necessary start off, to add their quota to the work of the World on a scale not inferior to that of the average white man. The time is long past due to right the wrongs perpetrated against my people, and no government could act speedily enough in making real their promises of long standing.

In conclusion, let me assure you that I have addressed these remarks to you in the interests of justice and truth and I am confident that you will accept them in the same spirit.

I remain, Dear Sir John,

Gratefully and sincerely yours

P.S. This is a copy of an open letter to the Times, London, which, I hope may be published in true explanation of the state of affairs here and in appreciation of the good work of your society on our behalf.

58. William Cooper, Secretary, Australian Aborigines' League, to church leaders, 27 December 1937, petition to His Majesty

You will be aware, from the references in the press, that the aborigines have presented a petition to His Majesty King George, praying the exercise of the Royal Prerogative to —

> "prevent the extinction of the aboriginal race and to give better conditions for all, granting us the power to propose a member of Parliament, of our own blood or a white man known to have studied our needs and to be in sympathy with our race, to represent us in the Federal Parliament".

This petition was signed by 1814 natives from every State, excepting Tasmania, where none of our people remain, and from the Commonwealth Territories. Many more would have signed but for the fear of reaction to their disadvantage and many of these would sign now if the petition were in course of preparation.

We have been approached by many who have suggested that we should organise a petition of white men praying for the same relief for aborigines. Of course the Organisation of such an appeal is beyond our resources and so we submit the following for your consideration: —

If you are favorable to the request, would you, as the Head of your Denomination, write to the Prime Minister in support. Would you kindly forward the matter for the consideration of the ministers of your denomination, requesting that, if they are agreeable, they too should write in support. Then it may be possible that the various Churches connected with your denomination might be given an opportunity of expressing their opinion, which could be forwarded to the Prime Minister.

In this way the very definite public opinion of the Christian community, could be vocalised and the Government be made aware of its sincerity.

The present Federal Government has assured the natives of its sincere desire to do all possible to help them and have given an earnest [sign] of their good intentions by the issue of a policy far in advance of any previously contemplated. The support of the public will assure its implementation. Of course the Federal Government has only power to legislate for natives in the Territories but we are sure that this must inevitably lead to similar relief in the sphere of the States.

Thank you,
For and on behalf of the Australian Aborigines,
Yours sincerely

59. William Cooper, Secretary, Australian Aborigines' League, to the Premier, New South Wales, Bertram Stevens, 1 January 1938

In the name of the League I have to lodge a strong protest against the type of homes now being built at Cumeroogunja, both in respect of their size and the details of the buildings.

We have heard much for some time about the old camps, built under Government policy within the past few years in some cases, being condemned and being replaced by good homes. We expected that the homes would be better than the ones built 50 years ago but we now find them to be of only two rooms and built of mill rubbish. No windows are being provided but wooden shutters which, if open, will let in weather and if closed will shut out fresh air. While every authority is talking of removing slums Slums are being built at Cumeroogunja. While the papers are talking housing reform, the natives are to get hovels.

We protest that our people ought to be able to observe common decency. How that can be done with two rooms I can't imagine. Instead of brick chimneys we have tin ones. Frankly the dark people, educated during the last 50 years to appreciate the amenities of life, are to be pushed back into barbarous conditions.

While registering this complaint, we reiterate our previous representations about the sanitary system (or want of it). Nothing but sheer necessity will send a person to these abominable places. The pans get overfull and have no lids, so that being carted away the contents are spilled in the road.

We were being encouraged to expect something decent but it appears that we are to be dehumanised.

I do trust that you will have the work stopped till you can have the matter investigated and that then you will issue instructions for something better.

I remain,

Very sincerely yours

60. *Age*, 18 January 1938, 'Day of Mourning: Aborigines not in Sympathy'

The Minister for the Interior (Mr McEwen) has received, through Rev. J. H. Sexton, Honorary secretary of the Aborigines' Friends' Association, a letter from Dr David Unaipon, a full-blooded aborigine, in which Mr Unaipon, speaking for the aborigines of Australia, takes exception to the proposal that the opening day of the anniversary celebrations in Sydney should be regarded by Australian aborigines as a day of mourning. Mr Unaipon is an authority on native legends, on which he has written a book. Mr Sexton's letter reads: —

David Unaipon a well known native leader in Australia, a full-blooded aboriginal, and a prince of his tribe has asked me to forward you the enclosed letter for your information. He is not in sympathy with the day of wailing being staged in Sydney on Foundation day. He considers it will only harm Australia abroad, and he says you can make what use you like of his letter. David is the author of a booklet on native legends, and is a good speaker, with an excellent English vocabulary, is very gentlemanly in bearing, and, you will see by his message, a man of common sense. The wailing day will be availed of to criticize Governments and generally finding fault, instead of showing appreciation of the efforts being made to aid the aborigines.

Mr Unaipon's letter was as follows: —

This day of mourning is a huge mistake, because it is of political character. The movement is largely an emotional one, sponsored by sympathetic white people and half-castes in order to call attention to native grievances. But the 50,000 full-blooded aboriginals will have very little part in this matter. These will stoically and silently await the coming of a new day.

The signs of this are already on the horizon, for the Prime Minister of Australia has already promised a Commonwealth review of the position. The most effective way of bringing this about is not by traducing Australia and giving it a bad reputation abroad, but by expressing appreciation of what is being done and contemplated for the aborigines. The many hopeful signs of an awakening interest in the native races is a cause for rejoicing, rather than weeping. The most effective way of helping the natives is not in weeping and bemoaning the past, but by acting in the living present. There have been grave faults on both sides, causing misunderstanding and friction,

William Cooper's second wife, Agnes (née Hamilton), pictured in about 1900 with some of her and William's children. Amy is seated on her knee; Dan, killed during World War I, is on her left, Jessie and Gillison to her right. Emma, a daughter from Cooper's first marriage, is standing (Alick Jackomos)

July 16th 1933

adress W Cooper
120 Ballarat Road
Footscray
Melbourne

The rev J Gribble

Dear Sir

receiving a number of very unplesent reports about the cruelty to the aborigines in westren australia I became anxious about these Natives, and I feel it my duty to help to take up this cause for to ask for better treatment to the Aboriginal in general I have wrote a number of letters to diferent Mission station in Diferent parts of Australia. the names of the Missions is as fallow forest river yarrabah sherboury. point Maclaey. writing to Natives on all Missions is to Educate the Aborigines openions in this cause for the Betterment of our selves. we have suffered quit Enough. and the time as arrived for the Natives to receive better treatment. it is noticsable that Government are taking a Keener intrests in this cause for better. I must say that the right

William Cooper to Rev. Ernest Gribble, 16 July 1933 (Australian Institute of Aboriginal and Torres Strait Islander Studies)

Some residents of Cumeroogunga outside their church about the time of World War I. Thomas James is in the back row, fourth from the left, holding a Bible. Bruce Ferguson, manager of the reserve, stands next to him. James's son Shadrach, who received some notice in the Melbourne press in 1929 and 1930 for his outspoken criticism of his people, is in the middle row, second from the left. His sister Priscilla is seated at the organ (Alick Jackomos)

William Cooper tried to make contact with Aboriginal people throughout Australia, corresponding with Aborigines in the various states and making personal visits to reserves in Victoria and New South Wales. Here he is pictured at Framlingham, in the Western District of Victoria, with (standing, left to right) Henry McRae, William Austin, Jim Rose and Nicholas Couzens, and (seated) Mary Lancaster, Esther Couzens and Lucy McDonald (Alick Jackomos)

170 Ballarat Rd
Footscray W 11
Victoria   19 March 1934

M. H. Makin
Dear Sir,
　　Why can't Mr Bleakley give me Something definite, as regards my petitioning my own people for Signatures, in Queensland as each of the other States have done, it is just upon Six months since I first applied, & the enquiries of the attitude of the other States are still being put forward as the reason, Surely it does not take all that time to get an answer, other matters of less importance get more business action than this has, the whole matter is being held up, as my people do not want to do anything against the Board of Protection, yet are willing to sign so long as it will not offend.
　　If something decisive is not arrived at very Soon, greater publicity will be given to the unnecessary delay meted out by the Board, their duty is to help our race in a reasonable manner, as we are Subjects of the Realm.
　　In your reply dated 14 Dec 33 you Suggest, that if there is any objection raised, to apply to yourself or Some other member, will you please accept my appeal & try & help me. Thanking you in anticipation
　　　　　　　　　Yours Respectfully
　　　　　　　　　　W Cooper

In 1936 the Australian Aborigines' League sponsored a meeting, held at the Society of Friends' Meeting House, to coordinate the activities of groups concerned about the plight of Aboriginal people. A choir, comprising William Cooper, Margaret Tucker, William's son Lynch and his third wife, Sarah, sang at the meeting (Alick Jackomos)

The 1938 Day of Mourning. Doug Nicholls and William Cooper, seated, listen to Jack Patten read the resolution. The other men pictured are Tom Foster and Jack Kinchela, partly obscured (Jack Horner Collection, Australian Institute of Aboriginal and Torres Strait Islander Studies)

AUSTRALIAN ABORIGINES' LEAGUE

"A fair deal for the dark race."

WILLIAM COOPER,
Hon. Secretary

DOUG NICHOLLS,
Hon. Treasurer

43 Mackay Street,
SEDDON, W.11.,
Victoria,

June 25th 1937

The Hon. the Minister
for the Interior,
CANBERRA,

Dear Mr. Paterson,

    I do thank you for your willingness to discuss the matter of the aborigines with me by letter. It is but another token of your genuine desire to do the right by my people. You say my previous letter was in a pessimistic strain. Mr. Paterson, I am an old man and I did hope to live to see my people in a fair way to uplift. My hopes are not being realised, hence my despair. If my claims for my people are just, why should I not look for immediate relief. If they are unreasonable cannot I claim to be shown in what way they are. I am being assured all round that what we ask is only our right and therefore I feel that I am right when I persistently press for this right.

    I am delighted at the assurance that your colleagues in the Federal Cabinet are likeminded with you and the Prime Minister in sincere desire to do the very best by our people.

    I understand that the Federal Parliament has jurisdiction only over such aborigines as may live in the Territories. There are over 18,000 full bloods in these parts and I venture the opinion that if the Federal Government deals adequately with the problem as it affects the aborigines under its control a definite lead will be given to the State Governments and a favorable psychology will be developed in the general public.

    Mr. Paterson, your kindness is so genuine that I feel I can respectfully say to you, without impropriety, that you should, just for the moment, forget that you are a white man so that you may look at the matter as we do. To see things as we do, to feel as we do, is the best way to realise the extent of our disabilities. We do not want our people to remain primitive, uncultured and a prey to all comers. Why should we remain in the near Stone Age ? The British were once where we are now. The conquering power of Rome, whatever else it did, lifted the British to culture and civilisation. We want that same uplift. Are we unreasonable ?

    We have proven our capacity, all over Australia, to become capable in every form of husbandry. In places we have made ourselves indispensable. We have acquired the faculty for the arts

William Cooper to Thomas Paterson, 25 June 1937 (National Archives of Australia)

AUSTRALIAN
Aborigines Conference

SESQUI-CENTENARY

Day of Mourning and Protest

to be held in

THE AUSTRALIAN HALL, SYDNEY

(No. 148 Elizabeth Street — a hundred yards south of Liverpool Street)

on

WEDNESDAY, 26th JANUARY, 1938

(AUSTRALIA DAY)

The Conference will assemble at 10 o'clock in the morning.

ABORIGINES AND PERSONS OF ABORIGINAL BLOOD ONLY ARE INVITED TO ATTEND

The following Resolution will be moved:

"WE, representing THE ABORIGINES OF AUSTRALIA, assembled in Conference at the Australian Hall, Sydney, on the 26th day of January, 1938, this being the 150th Anniversary of the whitemen's seizure of our country, HEREBY MAKE PROTEST against the callous treatment of our people by the whitemen during the past 150 years, AND WE APPEAL to the Australian Nation of today to make new laws for the education and care of Aborigines, and we ask for a new policy which will raise our people to FULL CITIZEN STATUS and EQUALITY WITHIN THE COMMUNITY."

The above resolution will be debated and voted upon, as the sole business of the Conference, which will terminate at 5 o'clock in the afternoon.

TO ALL AUSTRALIAN ABORIGINES! PLEASE COME TO THIS CONFERENCE IF YOU POSSIBLY CAN! ALSO SEND WORD BY LETTER TO NOTIFY US IF YOU CAN ATTEND

Signed, for and on behalf of

THE ABORIGINES PROGRESSIVE ASSOCIATION,

J. T. PATTEN, President.
W. FERGUSON, Organising Secretary.

Address: c/o. Box 1924KK, General Post Office, Sydney.

The flyer and poster advertising the Day of Mourning in Sydney to mark the sesqui-centenary of British settlement (Anti-Slavery Society)

William Cooper and the Australian Aborigines' League's attempts to improve conditions on Cumeroogunga achieved little beyond victimisation of its residents. This photograph of the Church of Christ Sunday School was taken on the reserve about 1938. Pastor Eddie Atkinson is standing third from the left, his wife, Ellen, is in the centre row, also third from the left. Their co-religionists, the Paynes, who were friends of Arthur Burdeu, stand at opposite ends of the back row (Alick Jackomos)

Pictured here are some of the Australian Aborigines' League's left-wing supporters on the road from Melbourne to Barmah in about March 1939, taking supplies to those who had walked off Cumeroogunga the previous month. George Patten is second on the left, standing next to Helen Baillie (Alick Jackomos)

and the exclusion of natives from the Federal constitution intensified the problem, because this left a national concern to be handled by State Governments.

As a representative of the race, I would like to urge that the 150th anniversary of Australia should be celebrated by the inauguration of a new programme, by which all the privileges of the dominant race should be given to the blacks. The time is past to talk of segregation. Let my people come more fully into the national family. There have been enough scientific investigations already, and no new facts have been brought to light, and yet there is still a plea to segregate the natives, keeping them in practically bush museums for scientific purposes.

The natives should not be kept in the cradle any longer. The aborigines want to be released from the ties that bind them to a decayed system, and want to be associated practically with the whites in the development of Australia, and they ask that the 150th anniversary of the continent may be marked by the wiping off of old scores and the inauguration of a worthy national programme for the promotion of their well being.

61. William Cooper, Secretary, Australian Aborigines' League, to the Minister for the Interior, John McEwen, 19 January 1938

At an executive meeting of this league held last evening, considerable perturbation was caused by the fact that the press of yesterday contained references which, if left unnoticed, might be prejudicial to our organisation. Though we do not know if it was so, the report of the Age left the impression that you had communicated the matter to the press. This report said, inter alia, "the 'wailing' day will be availed of to criticise governments and generally finding fault, instead of showing appreciation of the efforts being made to aid the aborigines".

You will know that this league has always been most courteous and appreciative. We have again and again told Mr Paterson and the Prime Minister that we were thoroughly seized of their good will. We have always felt that we had too good a cause to have to resort to any other policy and the years of our dealings with the Federal Government and State Governments has proved the wisdom of our method. We have never let up on our claim for equality and never ceased to protest at any proposed adverse action but we have always kept our hands and pen clean. This your colleagues well know. We do not intend to depart from our practice. We are buoyed up with the knowledge that our cause must triumph and with the assurance that the present Federal Government desires this.

As to the day of mourning. This is but a protest to our white fellow Australians. There is nothing ulterior and we are not able to appreciate how any reasonable person could twist the matter as has been done.

We try to keep from personalities and replying in the same way as we are criticised but I must say that David Uniapon never did and does not now occupy any place of leadership among the natives. We have felt that his great ability could have been used to help his people but this task has had to be assumed by those of inferior capacity and opportunity. The day of mourning does have the support of aborigines who are advanced enough to understand it and Mr Uniapon will not have enough company of antis to keep him warm.

We know that you will appreciate all I have said and will sensibly understand both the need for the protest and the manner of it.

I enclose a copy of a memorandum sent [to] the head of every denomination in Australia which will show the spirit in which this league approaches the Day of Mourning and the Sesqui-Centenary.

As there is no matter in my letter that demands a permission from you to allow [it] to be published, I have supplied a copy of this letter to the "Age" newspaper only for the reason that if we waited the advantage of a reply would have no value. We trust that you will approve our action. We feel that the adverse comment following the dropping of a spanner in our machinery by one who should know better demands early action ...

Australia Day 1938: Aborigines' Day of Mourning

The Australian Aborigines' Progressive Association of New South Wales has called on all aborigines in the advanced stages of civilization and culture to observe a DAY OF MOURNING concurrently with the white man's DAY OF REJOICING to celebrate the 150th year of the coming of the white man to Australia. The aborigines, by this means, hope to call the attention to the deplorable condition of all aborigines, of whatever stage of culture, after 150 years of British rule. It is expected that such action will create such sympathy on the part of the whites that full justice and recompense will follow.

The "DAY OF MOURNING" has been endorsed by the Australian Aborigines League, the Victorian body, which also looks after Federal matters, and it is expected that meetings will be held in a number of places and suitable resolutions passed. The League now asks the Christian community to help us in another way: —

We know that sympathy with the aborigines is widespread and growing, and, because the aboriginal knows that the goodwill of the white man is essential to success they seek to justify the continuance of this sympathy. We now ask all Christian denominations to observe Sunday, 23rd January, as *ABORIGINES' DAY*. We request that sermons be preached on this day dealing with the aboriginal people and their need of the gospel and response to it and we ask that special prayer be invoked for all missionary and other effort for the uplift of the dark people.

We regret the unavoidable delay in submitting our request, which was not avoidable in all the circumstances, but we feel that a suitable notice from you in your church press will give that wide publicity that is so essential.

62. William Cooper, Secretary, Australian Aborigines' League, to the Minister for the Interior, John McEwen, 19 February 1938

Mr E. E. Kramer has explained to me his proposals re the ration depot at Alice Springs and the natives who are not in employment there being removed to a suitable location where there is sufficiency of native food. I am thoroughly in accord with the proposal and would like to explain the policy of our league in that connection.

We feel that the natives should be educated and civilised on their own reservations so that they will ultimately be able to take their places in civilised society as valuable units. We appreciate that little can be expected from the present generation who should be allowed to live their own lives as largely as possible, but we do feel that a definite policy of uplift should take the young people and fit them for the civilisation of the white people. We therefore suggest:

1. That the people not in employment be removed from Alice Springs to the suitable location mentioned. That the location be an aboriginal station as is the practice in more advanced parts, as Palm Island. That a Manager be placed in Control to organise the young natives, and the old ones to the extent they are willing, in the development of a portion of the land according to its capacity by up to date methods. Certain of the area should be used to stock with cattle, etc. so that our idea of making the native settlements self-supporting can be tried out. It should be possible to do this without immediately displacing the native animals which are the normal food of natives. In short that a policy be framed to take the native as he is and bring him to the full culture of the white. There should be educational facilities for the children. CANNOT THE GOVERNMENT REGARD THIS AS A GOOD PLACE FOR AN EXPERIMENT WHICH SHOULD BE SYMPATHETICALLY CARRIED OUT AND WHICH MAY, ACCORDING TO THE EXPERIENCE GAINED, BE A PATTERN FOR FUTURE WORK. WE SAY, QUITE DEFINITELY, THAT ABORIGINAL UPLIFT SHOULD BE SELF-LIQUIDATING AND THE GOVERNMENT POLICY SHOULD BE BASED ON THIS COMMENDABLE PRINCIPLE.

I do trust that you will be able to meet the wishes of Mr Kramer, of many years experience in those parts and a man who regards us as human beings capable of thorough culture.

Might I suggest that while you are in the Territories you call at Bonny Well, the Station of Mr Curtis, south of Tennants Creek. You will there see aboriginal capabilities given full expression. We want you to see that we are practical and that when we make claims we are not merely theorists. We want also to impress that it is white interests that will be served as well as aboriginal when the problem which is not insoluble is properly tackled. May I summarise Aboriginal claims in a few sentences:

    1. Aborigines are entitled to a quid pro quo for the loss of their lands and liberty. This is implied in the term BRITISH JUSTICE. If the aborigines are merely a conquered and enslaved people it is not consonant with British principle.

    2. Aborigines do not ask Charity but Uplift. They ask for full equality in law but also the opportunity to qualify for it. Aboriginal uplift can be made self-liquidating and it ought be.

    3. Aborigines must not be an exploitable cheap labor but they must be fully equipped to serve Australia and should ultimately be living under Australian conditions. When the aboriginal people are fully cultured and are Australian in the fullest sense of the term you will be proud of us.

    4. There is that transitionary period. A policy, longsighted and sympathetic, must be framed and carried out to bring the aboriginal over in the shortest time and the most thorough fashion.

    5. NO OUTWORKING OF THE WHITE AUSTRALIA POLICY SHALL WORK DETRIMENTALLY TO THE NATIVES. FOR THE PURPOSES OF THIS POLICY, THE ABORIGINAL IS WHITE. (IS NOT THAT REASONABLE?) WE BELIEVE AND CONTEND THAT ABORIGINES, NOT SOUTHERN EUROPEANS, ARE THOSE WHO SHOULD DEVELOP THE OUTBACK. WE CAN DO IT, UNDER WHITE GUIDANCE, BETTER THAN ANY OTHERS FOR THE CLIMATE HAS NO TERRORS FOR THOSE WHO HAVE NEVER KNOWN A MORE FAVORABLE ONE. WE CLAIM THAT THE PEOPLING OF AUSTRALIA'S UNSETTLED AREAS WITH CIVILISED ABORIGINES IS THE BEST WAY TO CLOSE AUSTRALIA'S BACK DOOR FOR THE ABORIGINAL IS LOYAL AND EFFICIENT.

    TRY US OUT! WE LOOK TO YOU. WE HAVE NOWHERE ELSE TO TURN.

    Yours sincerely

63. William Cooper, Secretary, Australian Aborigines' League, to the Prime Minister, Joseph Lyons, 31 March 1938[60]

I am sending you the enclosed which I have compiled to give the aboriginal mind on the problem of the Native race. I will be glad if you will consider this because I feel very disappointed from time to time with the public statements by White men, made with all good intention, no doubt, but which, written from the point of view of the white man, does not reflect the opinions of natives.

From an educated black

Believing that there is a spark of human kindness in nearly every heart and knowing that the vast majority of men are opposed to oppression, I think that the majority of Australians, and British people in general, need only KNOW what my people have suffered and are suffering, to bring the relief long sought and now much overdue. Hence this letter.

My earnest ambition always has been to publish abroad the truth about my people, the Australian Aborigines, in order that the white people might know something of the facts concerning the treatment of my race.

I have addressed numerous letters to the editors of the various newspapers and find that my pleas for better conditions are, in nine cases out of ten, "pigeon-holed".

In spite of this fact we live in the hope that some day the newspapers will begin to publish the truth concerning Aboriginal affairs so that the public, being informed, will see that the great evils from which we are suffering are remedied.

Failure to publish letters which seek to lay before the public the truth concerning aboriginal conditions is as unfair to the public as it is to the aborigines. Additionally it is very inconvenient to the Aborigines who are forced to seek other channels to get information through to sympathetic white friends. The whites are starved for want of the facts on the subject. The blacks suffer through this starvation. Thus the newspapers contribute to the plight of both parties.

We Aborigines are a "protected" people. I understand that the correct meaning of the word "Protector" is: — "One who protects from injury — one who protects from oppression; a guardian; a regent; one who rules for a sovereign".

It would please us greatly to have a protector over our people who would live up to that standard but how do our protectorates work? Sometimes there is a measure of kindness shown to us, more often there is not. Take for instance the policeman who was appointed as a protector of the Aborigines in Central Australia. He went out one day to arrest a native who was reputed to have killed a white man.

He stated in his evidence that he shot 17 natives, and later shot another 14, and a so called "Justice of the Peace" officially without a trial justified the constable for shooting these 31 people. Now, I ask you, do you think that this Justice of Peace could justify the Constable before God?

Do you think that he could justify his own judgment before the King? No! The whole thing is contrary to British Justice and cannot be justified even before a much lower tribunal, the white people, (if they knew the facts) and of these, you are one!

History records that in the year 1771 white men first landed on the shores of what is now called Botany Bay. They claimed that they had "found" a "new" country — Australia. This country was not new, it was already in possession of, and inhabited by, millions of blacks, who, while unarmed, excepting spears and boomerangs, nevertheless owned the country as their God given heritage.

From the standpoint of an educated black who can read the Bible upon which British constitution and custom is founded, I marvel at the fact that while the text book of present civilization, the Bible, states that God gave the earth to man, the "Christian" interferes with God's arrangement and stops not even at murder to take that which does not belong to them but belongs to others by right of prior possession and by right of gift from God.

In our primitive state we Aborigines were gentlemen. Many of our present vices and defects have been imported. In our primitive state blacks were never known to take their own lives. No full blooded aboriginal ever went insane. We never had any sexual perverts in our midst, and we can proudly say that our moral standard was second to none and can take pride of place with the white people of our day.

While it is true that many of the whites who were sent here after the colony had been opened up were unjustly convicted and over-severely punished, it is also true that there were many criminals of the worst type let loose in our land and without doubt it was very unfortunate for us Aborigines to come into contact with the worst side of civilisation. This contamination has been detrimental to us.

Every shape and form of murder, yes, mass murder, was used against us and laws were passed and still exist, which no human creature can endure. Our food stuffs have been destroyed, poison and guns have done their work, and now white men's homes have been built on our hunting and camping grounds. Our lives have been wrecked and our happiness ended. Oh! ye whites!

The animals at the Zoo are looked after. They have servants to care for them. Food is supplied for them. Their homes are sure. Not so the blacks. We still feel unsafe in the hands of those who are controlling and "protecting" us. We still meet people who, with their sense of British superiority, look down upon us with disdain as unworthy of consideration — as "Abos", a race of another color — whereas the two races should be on the best of terms and give to each other full credit for the good qualities of which they are possessed.

Although usually treated with marked indifference, when we are not being ill-treated, there are times when we are considered useful. For instance, at least a thousand Aborigines were among the first to enlist in the defence of the British Empires in the 1914–18 war and for which Empire they gave their lives.

It was a thankless task for them, no thanks being given for the valuable services rendered. We get no encouragement, and the result of this neglect appears to be that we are looked upon as a useless race and greatly misrepresented thereby. This condition is to my mind due to State control, and so long as it exists the Aborigines will never be a valuable asset to their country.

I fear that these conditions will remain as they are until the Christian organisations, and other sympathetic friends, come forward with a definite determination to help to uplift these much down-trodden and broken people. We have never had the opportunity to prove that we can make good citizens and be useful to the country under white men's rule. We were good "citizens" when we owned the country.

All of us had plenty of food; no one starved while others had more than they could use. We had no depressions. Cancer, syphilis, and consumption were all unknown to us. They belong to the white civilisation. Our wives were OUR wives, and our morals without reproach. We WERE good citizens. We can adapt ourselves to the present arrangement and make good citizens NOW if we only get the chance.

If we are a burden on the country it is not our fault, but it is due to the fact that the various governments have not adopted the various practical suggestions which have been offered from time to time by men who know, including myself. Any lack of good citizenship on our part is due to the ill-considered and impracticable methods adopted when dealing with us.

It appears to me that because the governments have, to date, failed to view the life of the aborigines as the Aborigines see it themselves, we still find them crying for "protection", although what is really needed is "understanding" [...] Our millions have vanished [...] there are seventy thousand of us left [...] we are a dying race [...] Will you let us die?

Those of our people who are educated are becoming greatly concerned about the disabilities of the others and are putting up a stiff fight to try and get our people their rights. We still continue to try to persuade the Governments to do the right thing and appeal to all Christian people to view the matter with compassion and do their utmost, as opportunity arises, to try and help the Aborigines throughout the continent to get their rights, to get TRUE PROTECTION, and thus enable the race to continue and not become extinct.

Up to the present, petitions, deputations, requests, and other means and movements on our behalf have failed, so far as the Commonwealth Government is concerned.

Scientists, anthropologists and other distinguished gentlemen have also failed to bring relief, and we don't like being kept merely as material for scientific investigation, research, etc. etc. That is all valueless so far as the blackfellows' present needs and comforts are concerned.

Sending anthropologists into isolated parts of the continent amongst wild people with the object of doing the blacks good may have its scientific value, but after all, there are very few scientists in our midst to appreciate the scientists' point of view, whereas from our point of view it is a failure. It does not help the black fellow one little bit.

We suggest that the proper method of dealing with the primitive people would be to send educated and cultured Aborigines to their own uncivilized people. These men, of the same blood, would understand their people and would be able to suggest to the government means whereby the hardships and sufferings of these people could be alleviated or removed.

Up to the present we have not been given an opportunity to help our less fortunate brethren in their hard struggle, because we have been left homeless and penniless.

Many of us have not been given the right to vote. We have no right to vote. We are not even counted. We are not recognised as British subjects and have therefore no rights, and are unable to defend ourselves.

The Maoris of New Zealand have had parliamentary representation since 1867 and can place their grievances before the authorities through their representatives. Parliamentary representation for us has been refused. The inane reason advanced for the refusal being "it is unconstitutional".

In the early days the land was forcibly taken from the Maoris in some instances. In other instances it was "traded". A few axeheads for instance, were traded for thousands of acres of the best land in the Bay of Plenty district. Today, through legislation and negotiation, the descendants of those from whom the land was first taken or obtained have been and are being financially compensated for their loss, and rightly so. How much compensation have we had? How much of our land has been paid for? Not one iota! Again we state that we are the original owners of the country. In spite of force, prestige, or anything else you like, morally the land is ours. We have been ejected and despoiled of our God-given right and our inheritance has been forcibly taken from us.

As for ourselves we are a fast diminishing and dying race.

The time is long overdue when the Aborigines should be considered as much and as fully under the protection of the law as any other citizen of the Empire, and equally entitled to the privileges of British citizenship.

This more particularly in view of the fact that history records that in the commission originally given to those who came from overseas the strict injunction was given that the Aborigines and their descendants had to be adequately cared for.

This benevolent intention of his most gracious Majesty towards his primitive people was not carried out. We, therefore, now plead for moderation and forbearance to be exercised by all people in their dealings with the native people, and hope that the Government will seize every opportunity to carry out His Majesty's original intention to facilitate our approach toward civilization.

When we learn of these instructions given, and know the history of the manner in which we have been treated these last 150 years, our confidence in the professed Christian nation — standing for good government justice, and freedom — is sadly shaken. Nevertheless, we pledge ourselves to be loyal citizens of the Commonwealth of Australia, and believe that, as a people, we should be dealt with by the Commonwealth Government and NOT by the States. The States cannot return us a reasonable compensation without Commonwealth aid, so why not deal with us direct? Surely the Commonwealth, which controls all that originally belonged to us, could make what would be a comparatively meagre allowance for us, by way of recompense.

The taking of our rightful belongings has not yet ceased. A large percentage of hard-earned Aboriginal wages is even now handed over to the government and placed in the bank for the Aboriginals, in the "Aboriginal Trust Account".

Those wages amount to somewhere around a quarter of a million stirling and we have no knowledge regarding how we shall receive the benefits of this money. It is a mystery to us, who own[s] it. We think that the Aborigines should be transferred to the National authorities for Federal Control. We are glad that the Lyon's government has done something and that Mr Patterson, the Minister for the Interior, has shown some interest in our people.

Until now, in Federal Quarters, and still in other State Political circles, interest in the Aboriginal has been very nominal with all Administrations, or, at least, interest was merely of a scientific nature.

The only knowledge the native had of the Administration was the Iron hand of the Law he did not understand. The recognition of the aborigine as a human being is, so far as it yet applies, but of recent date. Interest in the aboriginal generally is daily more evident and conditions for the dark race seem to be more hopeful than ever before.

The change is most noticeable but nowhere so much as in the Federal Governmental sphere. For the first time in history the will to do a fair thing is evident and we trust that this good-will will work out for our emancipation.

Mr Lyons is kindly disposed and assured me that his cabinet share the same interest, but the Minister for the Interior, Mr Patterson who is responsible for Native Affairs, manifests an anxiety to do the utmost for us.

Communications with him have not been merely courteous (this is more and more the nature of all communications from each administration) but they have been kindly and considerate, resulting partly, from our representations, and he has asked his officers to investigate the whole position.

Already announcement of a programme has been made, and, though nothing material has yet been done, we trust that the wards of the Federal Government will shortly be on the way to full uplift.

This must inspire State Administrations and it appears that we have reason to feel that the Day of Hope is already dawning. When the uplift is materially advanced our promise of being a loyal, capable people, for which the outback is no problem, will be shown to be no vain promise and in the day the open back door to invasion will begin to close. The dark folk have not failed to tell the Prime Minister and Mr Patterson how deeply grateful they are for the good-will they are showing. But let us now get back to present realities.

The State has no useful work for us to do, and no educational move has been made to incorporate our people in national industry. It is unfair to treat us as a people of low mentality with treacherous tendencies who cannot be taught anything. We don't want to be kept living in captivity on Aboriginal settlements under the management of a retired policeman. In the sight of God we are as valuable as other men, and we feel sure that we could be taught, and we merely ask for an opportunity to prove that we can.

The treatment meted out to us has been so bad that the present generation of blacks lives in a state of fear and horror. The mass murders of the past, the prohibitions and restrictions of the present, and the dismal prospect of the future do not tend to bring out the best in us.

We suggest that we be placed under FEDERAL care, that we be dealt with via Christian Bodies, and educated blacks and half-castes, who know the view point of the blacks be used as contact men, and that by treating those now living, kindly the fear will be removed from the rising, and the next generation and that the generations following will prove that the time and money spent on their education was worth while.

Who better could deal with the great problems of the Northern Territory than an educated race of aborigines. The Aborigines have brains. These brains need cultivating.

It can be done. Will you do it? The aborigines have human affections which can respond to human treatment. Will they get it? Finally, do you intend to become as culpable as our original despoilers? Are you like the prominent Parliamentarian who, as late as 1935 said "The nigger has got to go, the sooner the better".

Will you, by your apathy tacitly admit that you don't care, and thus assume the guilt of your fathers? Are you prepared to see a race of people, without whom the centre and north of Australia can never be brought under human control, die and become extinct while you stand by and do nothing.

OR — are you prepared to admit that, since the Creator said in his Word that all men are of "one blood", we are humans with feelings like yourselves in the eyes of Almighty God, that we have joys and our sorrows, our likes and our dislikes, that we can feel pain, degradation, and humiliation just as you do? If you admit that, will you like true men do your bit to see a great injustice at least mollified by agitating for us to get a fair deal before it is too late?

I feel that the time has arrived for me to express the appreciation of my race for the increasing kind regard being shown by so many of the white race, and I take pleasure in doing so. Many of the present generation of white people are so sympathetic that I feel sure that the justice we are fighting for, and rightly desire, is coming. This is of particular value because it must be recognised that all the goodwill of the best of our Parliamentary leaders cannot avail as it should unless there is behind them the goodwill of the people.

64. William Cooper, Secretary, Australian Aborigines' League, to the Premier, Western Australia, 19 May 1938

At a meeting convened by this league and attended by hundreds of white citizens the following resolution was unanimously adopted:

That this meeting of Victorian citizens criticises the Government of Western Australia for the deplorable conditions existing amongst Western Australian aborigines and half castes, particularly the half-castes in the South West, where only a very small percentage of children are receiving any education whatever and the ration allowance for adults is valued at less than 1/- per week.

This meeting also urges that proper educational facilities be immediately established and that the Franchise, full sustenance allowance and all other Social Services be granted without delay.

It recommends that the financing of aboriginal administration should be on a National basis.

The meeting was held on Yarra Bank, on the afternoon of Sunday, 8th instant, and was well attended by unionists who also passed a motion calling on all Trades Unions to support the claims of aborigines.

Faithfully yours

65. William Cooper, Secretary, Australian Aborigines' League, to the Prime Minister, Joseph Lyons, 23 May 1938

Re our petition to the King for a representative in Parliament in respect of which there was considerable press publicity some months ago, which we believed to be inspired.

We are much concerned with the fact that there is now no further comment and no word from you in the matter. Would you please tell us how it now stands.

There have been statements that the whole matter of Aboriginal Administration is being referred to another conference of Premiers but not having heard of this either we wonder if that has also been abandoned. We certainly were perturbed about two matters, one being in the minutes of the conference of Chief Protectors to the effect that advice was being sought in America and South Africa on the problem as there existing and the other was from your Department to the effect that the Commonwealth was seeking to induce the States in the way of initiating legislation similar to the iniquitous legislation recently enacted in Western Australia. In the matter of the first we trust that there will not be copying of the shocking treatment of the natives in either place. Here, if we have the money we are allowed to ride in trams and walk on footpaths and, in the civilised parts, white men will treat colored women as women. Cannot our legislators evolve a scheme for Australia and cannot that scheme be that every civilised man and woman, full blood or half caste shall have full equality in law. Why should we be legislatively considered as we were when the white man came to our shores. Is there no time that we can look forward to when we shall be fully human in the eyes of white legislation?

The second matter, the suggested legislation in all States on the lines of the Western Australian legislation. We feel quite definitely that the white community here would not stand for the degradation of the native here as he has been degraded in West Australia in the last months. There men who were educated and have been in the enjoyment of the franchise for quarter of a century are declared aboriginals. They may not now give their daughters in marriage without in every case receiving the personal consent of the Commissioner for Native Affairs. They may not go to Perth without a permit nor work for a white employer without securing a license at the price of £1 per year. For God's sake don't have us all pushed back to West Australian status but rather show that State that their retrospective legislation is foreign to Australian sentiment.

We fully trust you and your Government. We know we can look to you for justice but we are not so sure of the Administrative officers in the States who may be able, as in West Australia, to manipulate legislation to our detriment.

We are waiting most anxiously and will be glad of a word from you.

Yours sincerely

66. William Cooper, Secretary, Australian Aborigines' League, to the Premier, New South Wales, Bertram Stevens, 23 May 1938

I have just returned from Cumeroogunga, whither I went because of the many complaints I have received as secretary of the League. The result of my trip I have submitted in a series of letters, separate ones for each matter to facilitate early consideration.

I feel, Mr Stevens, that the day should be passed when my people should have to be asking for the removal of disabilities imposed on no other people, not even the children of aliens who happen to be born here. We are not now primitive and, given a chance, we can prove ourselves as capable as any other section of the Community. We want to be real Australians, loyal members of the Australian Commonwealth and we would ask that you now give consideration to the removal of all discriminating legislation. We feel sure that your trust of us will be wholly satisfactory and we shall take a place in the community that will make us a real asset. We can't avoid the disability of colour and the prejudice of the White people when we would come into competition with them, but equality in law would be something.

We have suffered but we do not wish to dwell on that. We have not got what we should, but we seek, by co-operation, full manhood and womanhood. It would be fine if your State were to advocate this ideal to the other States and then set the example of giving us full equality in law. The results will be the best advocacy of similar rights in other States.

I remain,

yours sincerely

67. William Cooper, Secretary, Australian Aborigines' League, to the Premier, Western Australia, 11 July 1938

At the Annual meeting of the Australian Aborigines' League the following resolutions were adopted:

1. "That this League expresses its protest against the recently enacted legislation of Western Australia in respect of Aborigines".

We feel that the position of our race has been worsened from the bad position it was in previously in Western Australia and this at a time when improvement is being effected in other parts of Australia.

2. "That the deplorable condition of aborigines in Western Australia calls for urgent relief, and, pending the adoption of a Federal policy for Aborigines, this meeting asks that a grant be immediately made to Western Australia by the Federal Government, the expenditure of such grant to be subject to supervision by the Federal Government".

We know that the fundamental cause of the bad position in W.A. is that the number of aborigines in relation to the white population is so much greater than in the Eastern States. We feel that aboriginal costs should be borne by the population of Australia on a per capita basis.

May we appeal to you, head of the Labor Government, for the amelioration of our lot instead of its being worsened and for a policy for aborigines consistent with the strong sympathy of the Labour movement in the Eastern States. Frankly we are not able to understand why the official attitude of a Government, representing the workers, should be so inconsiderate of those whose plight should call for the utmost sympathy and consideration.

Hoping to hear of some relief for our downtrodden brothers,

Yours sincerely

68. William Cooper, Secretary, Australian Aborigines' League, to the Chief Secretary or Minister for Native Affairs, Western Australia, 17 July 1938

At a meeting of this league held on Saturday the resolution as set out attached was adopted and in forwarding it I desire to say that we aborigines keenly feel the repressive legislation under which the condition of our race in Western Australia has been worsened. Conditions have always been worse in Western Australia than in the rest of Australia and while we did not think it was possible for them to be worse than they were we have found that they have been worsened. It passes our comprehension why a Labor Government could be the instrument of forging our chains to be heavier and at a time when the Federal Government (non-Labor) is steadily improving our conditions and the Labor Government in Queensland is showing deeper concern for our welfare. The Labor policy for aborigines in New South Wales surpasses everything else contemplated in Australia, yet Western Australian Labor is out Hitlering Hitler in the way of hounding a harmless and well meaning race and regimenting the religious teaching and education we are to receive. Frankly we do not believe that the legislation enacted and the regulations under the act are the will of labor and we plead that the whole matter be referred to the party with a request that Labor express its voice in the matter. We do feel confident in the result if this be done.

I remain, Yours sincerely…

Motion adopted at a meeting of the Executive of the Aborigines' League, held on Saturday, 16 July 1938.

Resolved that:

The Australian Aborigines' League, the organised voice of the Natives of Australia, having watched the trend of the repressive legislation in respect of aborigines in Western Australia and the regulations made under the act, with the serious effect of both on our people strongly protests against many features of the Act and the regulations particularly those prescribing:

1. The obligation of natives to seek a permit to visit Perth and to produce such permit on demand.

2. The obligation of natives to obtain a license to enable them to be eligible to work for a white man.

3. The intrusion of the Department for Native Affairs into the personal life of aborigines, requiring that it shall be consulted and its approval obtained before our girls are allowed to be married to men of mutual choice.

4. The obligation of natives to cut adrift from their own kith and kin not exempted from the operations of the Act in order that they may be eligible to obtain exemption from the operations of the act themselves.

We also strongly protest against the regulation requiring missionaries and educationalists to be licensed to preach to or educate our people and that licences which may be granted may be revoked at any time without the right of appeal from the decision of the Department. This we consider to be a menace to the right of Free speech, hampering our friends in their stand for justice for our people.

We further consider that too much power is vested in one person, the Commissioner for Native Affairs, and we advocate the formation of a Board for the Protection of Aborigines, on which our people shall have representation.

We appeal for the vetoing of the Regulations made under the Act and the amendment of the Act itself to enable the removal of obnoxious clauses and we call on all people who love justice to stand by our people in their present need.

A copy of this resolution is to be sent to the Hons. the Minister for Native Affairs in Western Australia and the Minister for the Interior, Canberra.

69. William Cooper, Secretary, Australian Aborigines' League, to the Minister for the Interior, John McEwen, 26 July 1938

I have been deeply concerned about the policy for aborigines and particularly in respect of the reply to our petition to the King for representation in Parliament. From the replies to my correspondence I gather that nothing will be done in the matters of our concern till you return from the North and have drawn up the observations you will have to make in the matter. Because I feel that so much depends on your report I am taking the liberty of writing you asking that you frame your recommendations from the point of view of the interests of the natives. We are only too sensible of the White attitude in the North and, since you will have conferred wholly with those interests and seen the aboriginal problem only through a White Man's eyes we fear that you may be unconsciously biassed. I say this with every respect for you. I know you will do what you deem to be the right, fearlessly, but you cannot be expected to see the position through an aboriginal's eyes.

You will not have got the mind of the native, and the White men will probably have given you to understand that the native has not got one. But he has. He is not vocal, yet, but he is very definitely properly sensed of the injustice of his position. He is uncomplaining but don't take that to mean he has no complaints to make. He is human, please do remember that.

We aborigines feel we have a right to a place in Australia and, we feel we are robbed of that place. We do ask that place and quite definitely say that, Payne Commission Report and all other such policies, written or otherwise, [like] the White Australia policy is not just when it shuts out aborigines from the scope of the protection afforded by that policy. We claim that it is not British stock that is wanted for the Territory, certainly not Southern European but Aboriginal, British Australian aborigines. We claim that Australia, in the areas where the aboriginal is still numerous, should be developed for and by the aboriginal and it seems clear to us that we have proved our aptitude for primary industry so proving that it is not merely visionary when we talk of an aboriginal race, civilised, industrialised and bearing his share of responsibility for his country. *WE CLAIM THAT THE INSPIRATION FOR A POLICY FOR ABORIGINES SHOULD BE — "THE ABORIGINAL — AN ASSET".*

We don't want to be zoological specimens in Arnhem Land or in any other reservation, though we realise that reservations are essential for a long time yet. We don't want to be on charity. We want to be real men in our Own Australia, Loyal subjects of the Empire and the Commonwealth. Given a chance and a patiently worked out policy of Uplift, we will yet make Australia realise that we are an asset. Give us a helping hand out and you will get 90,000 units, more or less, to help Australia work out her destiny.

No Honest White man claims that we have had a fair deal or that the aboriginal problem (of the White man's making) is not capable of easy solution given the will to do right by us. We just ask what the White Man, in his heart, knows is bare justice.

This is where we need our member, able to watch legislation on the floor of the House, able to speak for the native and to represent native interests. We are of the opinion that if we had a good man devoted to our interests he could do more for our cause than "a majority" in Parliament. Though he would have no vote and be the stronger for that fact, he would be the most powerful factor in the House. We haven't got our member, YET, but we have friends and among them are the men who have been, and one now is, Minister for the Interior. In fact we feel that we have a majority in the House and would like to see this matter dealt with in a non-party spirit.

Do not misunderstand me when I sign myself in the words of our League motto, "For a Fair Deal for the Dark Race",

Yours sincerely

70. William Cooper, Secretary, Australian Aborigines' League, to the Prime Minister, Joseph Lyons, 10 September 1938

The letter from your Department, dated 8th August, re the natives at Cumeroogunga who had their names removed from the roll of electors has been noted with thanks. The reply, however, gives me the material for further representations which I make to you personally, knowing that you will give it favorable consideration so far as you are concerned.

The letter in question mentions that only two natives are not now on the roll, one of whom has since left the station. The sole full blood remaining, Fred Stewart, is better educated than most of the half-castes and is a good type whose only fault is that he has not an admixture of white blood, a detriment only in White eyes. By reason of his education and capacity he acted as clerk on the station when he was young. This coupled with the fact of other full bloods, whom we could name but whom you also know of, surely brings to notice the unreasonableness of the discrimination against full bloods. This I know you will agree with if there is no obstacle we are unaware of. Regardless of whether there is any such obstacle I do ask that you take the necessary steps to bring all natives, of full or half blood into the status of whites, in the conditions in which half-castes are brought in. This will involve not only the franchise but pensions as well. Surely at this late hour it is not too much to ask, even if special legislation has to be introduced.

Hoping for a favorable reply,
Yours sincerely

71. William Cooper, Secretary, Australian Aborigines' League, to Rev. William Morley, Secretary, Association for the Protection of Native Races, 5 November 1938

I was very interested to note in the press that the N.S.W. Government proposes to introduce legislation providing for the abolition of the present board and appointing another form of administration. This is good so far as it goes but a more real reform would remove the power of the managers and matrons, who in some cases, are ruthlessly persecuting our people. I can assure you that our natives are boiling over with indignity at the way the managers and matrons are oppressing us, often using the color of law to aid them. Did you know the full story your blood would boil. We therefore have asked the Premier to grant: —

1. Representation of aboriginal interests in the new administration. We want someone to whom we can look as one who will urge our viewpoint and whom we can contact in cases that we feel need being ventilated before the Board. An anthropologist does not fill the bill as you will appreciate.

2. Representation of the natives on the administration of the stations. We propose a council, appointed by the people who will have status and authority as a municipal council. This will relegate the Manager and matron into a place more approximating the Governor than a Dictator, a representative of the government, the administration and ultimately of the King, who is assured of native loyalty both to His Person, His Throne and His Government.

We want respect for the rights of minorities to be conceded in Australia just as much as Australia contends that this right be conceded to European minorities. In fact we dont want to be m[e]rely a minority but as Australians, as loyal as any other Australians, to be accorded the same status and rights that other Australians enjoy. This representation will be a step to our full emancipation.

With best wishes,
Yours sincerely

72. William Cooper, Secretary, Australian Aborigines' League, 'Native regulations: Aborigines' League Protest', letter to the Editor, *West Australian*, 22 November 1938

My attention has just been drawn to your issue of the 3rd inst., in which Mr Gray, M.L.C., commends the services of the Commissioner for Native Affairs (Mr Neville). Being in constant contact with Western Australia and having learnt from our own members of the condition of the natives, we were heartened when we learnt that the iniquitous and obnoxious regulations under the infamous legislation of Western Australia were to be dropped. To learn that they are not to be causes us dismay.

Rightly or wrongly, we regard the offensive legislation and regulations to be the inspiration of Mr Neville and absolutely contrary to Labour aspirations. Labour here is definitely favourable and sympathetic to native interests and the announced policy of New South Wales Labour forecasts the full emancipation of our people. When we tell Labourites here of the parlous condition of our brethren in the West and tell them of the un-British repression and persecution of the legislation and regulation, we are often met with the remark "and Labour is in power?" Cannot Labour see the folly of their Government's crucifixion of a harmless, defenceless people, for the blame must rest on the Government, even if it is only a rubber stamp in Mr Neville's office.

We are not satisfied with our conditions in any State, but in every one without exception, apart from Western Australia, there is the definite promise of improvement. With so much talk of the rights of minorities, which nearly involved Australia in war along with the rest of the Empire, it seems hard to believe that another minority can be ground to dust when it only wants the right to be loyal Britishers, sharing with their white brethren the privileges and responsibilities of citizenship.

One clause in your issue referred to surprises. We never hear Mr Neville quoted as an authority and would be surprised if we did. We have heard it said that he was merely a civil servant who was appointed to the office regardless of his want of experience. We have asked that the authority now vested in an officer who is not acceptable to our people be vested in a board and we contend that those constituting that board shall be either experts or representatives of interests which have regard for the native race. There should be women on that board and definite representation of the natives themselves. Cannot such a board be created? It would inspire the confidence the present administration fails to secure.

The plea of our league is "a fair deal for the dark race", otherwise a pogrom would be preferred to slow torture. Surely it is not beyond the capacity of the dominant race to deal with the trouble in such a way that we will be on the way to the removal of all talk of a native problem. We believe that a wise solution of the present difficult position will remove all problem[s] and will be as good as adding a new province to Australia.

Yours, etc.

73. A. P. A. Burdeu, President, Australian Aborigines' League, to the Minister for the Interior, John McEwen, 25 November 1938

We are hearing quite a lot of suggestions of late in respect of preparation for war, the empty North, population generally, and immigration. These all arise from Australia's preparedness for war and the consequences of unpreparedness.

No one seems to touch the real solution and Australia generally, does not seem to be aware of it.

Two things may be affirmed —

1. The empty North is Australia's heel of Achilles. Not a potential danger spot it is certainly the spot the enemy will strike at because no enemy could be resisted there.

2. A land hungry world will not suffer such land to lie idle while their millions lack elbow room.

Three other affirmations will not be contended —

1. Aboriginal reservations will only remain such till the land is wanted for other purposes, either by Australia or a country with eyes upon it, and in that day the Aboriginal will enter on the same blood bath his brothers have had to suffer unless definite arrangements to the contrary be made.

2. The Aboriginal is educable. He has proven this where there has not been any policy of Uplift. In fact, all Aboriginal attainment has been acquired not by plan, but despite the absence of one.

3. The Aboriginal loses his culture with the greatest facility. He as quickly acquires the culture of the superior race he contacts. (If that medium were foreign he would be a potential menace).

Cannot these matters be related and is not their relation the germ of an adequate solution of both the empty North and it's Aboriginal population. Let us further note —

1. The North is unsuitable for Nordic peoples, particularly women, for laborious effort, while it is the only country the Aboriginal ever knew and to which he is fully adjusted. Both white men and white women are able to live in the North in conditions that do not involve undue labor.

In the light of these facts, all of which are admitted, I submit that an Aboriginal policy should be formulated for the complete exploitation of the resources of the Territory by Aboriginal labor under white direction and oversight. Into this industrialization the young men and young women should be brought, for the persons now adult can scarcely be expected to respond. If the service is made attractive, it will attract and interest. Coupled with this industrialization, should be an educational policy for youth which can be made attractive and interesting. It is admitted that the task is not just as easy as "say so", but it should be obvious that if the native has been industrialized and somewhat educated without any policy, the implementation of a considered policy by experts, must be capable of much more.

And now for what has been misconstrued into my public utterances —

It has been crudely stated that I have suggested that natives should be put into khaki and used as soldiers. I never made any such ill-considered remark. What I did say and repeat is that the Aboriginal, civilized, industrialized, and emancipated, peopling the area which is home to him, will constitute a bulwark for the defence of the country, and in time of need he will be found ready to defend his country, and ours.

By this I obviously mean that if the Aboriginal is raised to full citizenship, he will assume the responsibilities of citizenship including defence, in parallel conditions with the white.

I would suggest that this is fully consonant with the policy of the Aborigines League, and should be given full consideration, as a matter of national importance. Such a policy will not be disruptive of any development of the Territory now being made, but being supplementary to that, to the extent that it is done, it must be advantageous.

Is it not apparent that the exploitation of Aboriginal possibilities is both advantageous to Australia and will add thousands to it's effective population?

We contend that the relation of two problems will solve both and neglect of these will aggravate both.

Yours sincerely

74. William Cooper, Secretary, Australian Aborigines' League, to the Chairman, Aborigines Protection Board, New South Wales, Sydney, 28 November 1938

While conditions in some parts of Australia are improving, for a long time I have been receiving complaints about conditions at Cumeroogunga. What impressed me was that complaints were made by men of sterling character, people of fine type. Some of the complaints I was not able to verify, not being on the spot and in respect of others I told those concerned that the League would have to have something definite before we could take up the matter. I felt that there was a good backing for some of the statements made but our league is careful in what it says and does not want to lose its good name by irrational statements. I wanted to be able to prove the statements made.

Later I received a petition, which I forward herewith, and which you will see is very representative of the people living on the settlement. On receipt of this I made personal enquiries and herewith is set out the complaints of the people. They are prepared to substantiate them to you personally or to a board of enquiry you may appoint. They are not satisfied that the Inspector (Mr Smithers) or some other officer conduct an informal enquiry. This in the past has never been satisfactory and it is as much a protest against such officers as against the management. They and this league ask for an enquiry which will seek to know facts with a view to a remedy.

1. The manager and the matron call all the married women only by their christian names. The married men object to this and the women support their protest. The women say that they are required to always call Mrs

MQuiggan Matron and they feel that she and the manager should call them Mrs Jones, or as the case may be.

2. Natives are not allowed under any circumstances to travel in the cab of the station truck. This rule is never varied, no matter what the weather, even with convalesents returning from the hospital. Native women, known to be tubercular, have been compelled to sit on the back of the truck, in the cold and wet, while there is room in the cab for these delicate people. The natives contend that the truck was supplied for the use of the station and that it is unreasonable to force delicate women out into the cold and wet while there is room in the cab for them.

3. The houses near the river do not get sanitary clearances though they are but a short distance from the centre of the township. The occupants bury the nightsoil. When the River rises over the land this nightsoil is disturbed and the water of the river is polluted.

4. The meat issued to the natives is from sheep so badly conditioned as to [be] fit only for boiling down. The carcasses average only 20 to 25 lbs. in weight. The meat is secured from the Echuca Freezer and is starving stock. It is unfit for human consumption and much is thrown to the dogs.

5. Many of those to whom clothing was issued under previous administrations do not now receive it which is now only issued to old people. A wider issue was made prior to Mr M'Quiggan being appointed.

6. The manner of Mrs M'Quiggan to the women is most offensive. She goes to the homes when she likes and says what she likes. If things don't suit her she bounces the women. If they pick her up for the way she speaks the rations are stopped or, if they are old people, their curry and pepper are stopped.

7. The natives ask that the Health Inspector visit the place and report on its condition.

8. Open night pans are infested with flies, which also pollute the food. A more suitable type of W.C. is necessary or, preferably, a septic tank system should be installed.

9. The streets are in bad order. In heavy rain, people are up to their knees in mud and water.

10. The rooms of the houses are too small and the number of rooms too few for the size of the families. Overcrowding results and there is much dissatisfaction.

The complainants are ready to submit evidence to a Board of Enquiry or yourself. They are not prepared to do so to the Inspector or other Officer of the Board responsible for the conditions.

The League supports the claim for a full, free and impartial investigation.

Yours sincerely

75. *Daily Telegraph*, 1 December 1938, 'Aboriginal Charges Cruelty'

At Cummeroogunya Reserve in the last 22 months the death-roll was six adults, four children, and fifteen babies died at birth, it was alleged yesterday.

Mr J. T. Patten, president of the Aboriginal Progressive Association, said that babies were dying of malnutrition.

"Mental and physical cruelty is inflicted by white men in charge of reserves," he continued.

"If orders are not obeyed, food supplies are stopped," declared Mr Patten, who is himself an aboriginal. "Aborigines are starved.

"Children are allowed meat once a week, with three onions and two potatoes.

"These rations are slowly exterminating the aborigines."

Reserves Leased

"Aborigines were granted 2900 acres. They are living on fourteen acres. The rest is leased to white men by the Aborigines Protection Board."

Mr Patten suggested that the 96 reserves in the State should be combined into one agricultural colony, worked by aborigines.

Abolition of Board

The association is asking for: Abolition of the Aborigines' Protection Board, full citizen rights for aborigines; repeal of the Aborigines Act; equal opportunities and education; facilities to work the land in reserves.

76. *Argus*, 7 December 1938, 'Deputation Not Admitted'

A deputation from the Australian Aborigines League which visited the German Consulate yesterday, with the intention of conveying to the Consul (Dr R. W. Drechsler) a resolution condemning the persecution of Jews and Christians in Germany, was refused admittance.

A letter requesting Dr Drechsler to forward the resolution to his Government was left at the Consulate.

The resolution, voiced "on behalf of the aborigines of Australia, a strong protest at the cruel persecution of the Jewish people by the Nazi Government of Germany, and asks that this persecution be brought to an end".

Delegates will attend the immigration conference called by the Council for Civil Liberties at the Assembly hall tomorrow night and on Saturday.

77. William Cooper, Secretary, Australian Aborigines' League, to the Minister for the Interior, John McEwen, Canberra, 17 December 1938

There have been copious extracts in the press which indicate that the long promised policy for aborigines has been issued. If this be so will you kindly let me have a complete copy so that I may fully examine it.

If these extracts are correct it would seem that there are, from our point of view, some blemishes which I trust you will be able to satisfy our aspirations on. One of these is discrimination between those of more than half aboriginal blood from those of half white or whiter color. This is our chief bone of contention over the years and is indicative of the white outlook on a problem in respect of which the dark people have quite a different opinion. I would like you to meet us in this respect, "Do not suppose that the colored folk have, generally, aspirations to be white or possess any regret as being colored". Do not therefore suppose that we feel any different toward any member of our race who is full blood as against one with some white blood. It may shock you to know that, very generally, even octaroons look with more sympathy on the aboriginal side of their ancestry than on the white side. There are exceptions, of course, but these prove the rule. The white man cannot "think black" but I submit that our chieftain, which is your particular position, and the Government, which is our guardian, should set themselves to learn to "think black". We speak thus to you only because we know in our hearts that you personally, and the Government of which you are a member, do want to do the right thing by us. We respect you, personally, and the Government, and repeat what we have told you before, and made no secret of publicly, that no Government previously has shown the same interest as the present Lyons Government in the natives. It is possible for us to ask of you what we want instead of being in the position of being suppliants for mercy from unsympathetic over lords.

What we ask is that fullbloods and near blacks be accorded the same opportunity to rise as half castes and near whites. Let the determination be, not color, but capacity. There are octaroons and quadroons unable to exercise the privileges of civilisation but there are full bloods who are fully able. Though you do not mean it, the discrimination shown by whites for those of partly white parentage is offensive and hurtful to colored people. Remove all barriers from the race to full progress and make our condition at least comparable to the person of alien blood who is born in the land. At present it is a stigma to be full blood or near black and yet the white man holds the land of our fathers without penny of compensation. This should not be and

I know it will not be ultimately but I should like to feel that the Magna Carta you are granting us does not retain the blemish I have referred to. You can, in one sweep, put us all on the same footing as the whites and super add the temporary conditions that will give the necessary help to the uncultured, near black or near white. Won't you do this? It will not cost a penny but if it did surely the debt of the white man to the dark one is not to be repudiated on the score of cost.

Mr M'Ewan, the white man has not yet shown any capacity for "thinking black". This is the whole position in a nutshell. Will you learn to do it?

We deeply appreciate your service to our race and cordially wish you, as you wish ourselves, the best of good wishes for the New Year ...

78. William Cooper, Secretary, Australian Aborigines' League, to the Minister for the Interior, John McEwen, Canberra, 17 December 1938

I have written to you generally on the subject of discrimination and have done so so that you might deal with the subject on the broad general lines of policy. I am writing to you separately on a specific matter so that you may be able to consider the matter apart from the general question, though it is very much related to it.

For years we have been seeking the removal of the reproach of color by the granting of pension rights and the maternity allowance. We did fully expect that we would have secured our long sought desire but a press announcement in the Argus of 8th inst. dashes our hopes to the ground. We are thoroughly disappointed and so feel that you do not fully appreciate the position.

We have near whites living under primitive or semi-primitive conditions. These have legal rights to full citizenship, which they cannot understand let alone exercise but *WE HAVE FULL BLOODS WHO ARE CULTURED ON THE FULL WHITE STANDARD.* What an indignity to have these branded as unfit to exercise the privileges of citizenship or to receive the benefits that accrue to the white person. We refrain from using names as a rule because dark folk have the same feelings as white people but what of David Uniapon and Rev. James Noble, full bloods, and christian gentlemen of education just to mention two who are famous. We can add to those names men of equal culture who are not so well known. What of little MENE, the child of 13 who won one of the Batman Essay Competition cups in the competitions recently carried out by the Uplift Society. Is he to grow up to be less than a man? We have even here in Victoria full blood natives and I call to mind one full blood family living here in Victoria, with the children in school with other colored children and whites for that matter. Some of these in this big family are just infants. Are they to grow up just different from those "favored" with white blood. This woman will get nothing for her maternity expenses but her neighbours get the bonus. In aboriginal eyes they are just the same as others and they live as others do on the "catch as catch can" basis. The most cultured christian gentleman who is not able to lay by sufficient for old age may not get a pension but must either go to an aboriginal station, there to queue up with all others to get the starvation issue that is given in most parts of Australia or have, if living privately to go to the police station for an even narrower ration. *If the white man wanted to think out an indignity for the man he has displaced, he could not do better than he has done by the natives.* We feel that while we are all indignant over Hitler's treatment of the Jews, we are getting the same treatment here and we would like this fact duly considered.

The Government has made its decision and we can quite understand the difficulties that presented themselves but they are more supposed than real. We do now definitely ask that there be added to this determination a proviso to this effect, "NOTWITHSTANDING THIS POLICY, ANY PERSON OF MORE THAN HALF ABORIGINAL BLOOD MAY BE BROUGHT INTO THE BENEFITS OF THOSE OF HALF WHITE BLOOD IF IT CAN BE PROVEN TO THE SATISFACTION OF THE MINISTER THAT THEY ARE COMPETENT TO EXERCISE OR ENJOY THESE BENEFITS. This is not in accordance with our claims but is a compromise. We claim that the full rights should be admitted in law and the persons not competent to exercise them should be excised and provided for otherwise.

I have mentioned previously in correspondence a story which will show how the gun is loaded against the person of mixed parentage and how many times this circumstance has applied nobody can say. One of our finest women, very dark complexioned, splendidly educated and who taught bible class in one of our white sunday schools for years, became ill. Her husband was only a laborer. She applied for an invalid pension. It was refused on the ground that her illness was not necessarily chronic. Later, she qualified in age for the old age pension and applied for it. She was refused as being obviously more than half native. Being able, possibly one of our most educated women, she appealed to the Prime Minister, who regretted that the law did not permit granting a pension. She then applied for State aid (she should be entitled to one or the other) but was told that as she was more than half white she was not entitled to state aid. When the woman was told the result, she remarked that "I am too black for a pension and too white for relief as a necessitous aboriginal". She got nothing and her death closed a case which if presented publicly would have brought matters to a head.

I would emphasise that what we are asking for the aboriginal born in Australia is already available to chinese, japanese, or other alien[s], if they happen to be born here.

May we claim the further attention we are seeking,
Yours sincerely

79. William Cooper, Secretary, Australian Aborigines' League, to Mr Kitson, the Chief Secretary, Western Australia, 30 December 1938

At a meeting held on 30th ultimo, the following resolution was adopted by this league, with membership in the different States and the responsibility for the interests of aborigines all over Australia:

That this meeting of the Australian Aborigines' League, on behalf of the aborigines of Australia, strongly criticises the attack on missionaries made by Mr Kitson.

While recognizing that regrettable episodes have occurred on some missions at various times, the league has intimate knowledge of the good work being done by the missionaries of all branches of the Christian church.

It is of the opinion that without the protection of missionaries our people would be much worse off, if not completely exterminated.

We therefore call on the Governments of Australia, particularly of Western Australia, to give greater moral and financial support to the missions of all denominations, thus enabling them to carry out constructive work for our people in cooperation with the Governments.

In forwarding this resolution let me reiterate that "we have never received anything of real value from any other source than missions, which are, and remain, our best friends".

Yours sincerely

80. William Cooper, Secretary, Australian Aborigines' League, to the Minister for the Interior, John McEwen, Canberra, 3 January 1939

I am writing to dissociate myself and the league from the published utterances of the President of the newly formed aboriginal organisation, the Aborigines' Progressive Association (Mr J. T. Patten).

Mr Patten has recently telegraphed the Western Australian Government on its attitude toward missionaries and missions, "our greatest enemies". This league has no such feelings against missions and feel that they have been and are our best friends. We fully approve of your reported appreciation of missions and the intention to implement your new native policy largely through missions.

Mr Patten has also advocated over the air the formation of aboriginal regiments. I am father of a soldier who gave his life for his King on the battlefield and thousands of colored men enlisted in the A.I.F. They will doubtless do so again though on their return last time, that is those who survived, were pushed back to the bush to resume the status of aboriginals. I feel that Mr Patten is previous in that the aboriginal now has no status, no rights, no land and, though the native is more loyal to the person of the King and the throne than is the average white he has no country and nothing to fight for but the privilege of defending the land which was taken from him by the white race without compensation or even kindness. We submit that to put us in the trenches, until we have something to fight for, is not right.

The enrolment of aboriginal regiments would of course prove that the aboriginal had some value but it would only be in the circumstance of the native levies of European countries, as, for instance, the Senegalese. It is the creation of a mercenary army not an army of men fighting for all that is dear in life.

My point, Mr M'Ewan, is that the enlistment of natives should be preceded by the removal of all disabilities. Then, with a country to fight for, the aborigines would not be one whit behind white men in value. Can you not get my point. Can we not have a "Balfour declaration" for natives of a national home in Australia. It will cost nothing to give the native born in the land the same right, not merely of the persons of European blood, but of Maoris and people of Chinese, Japanese or other Asiatic peoples, who may happen to be born in Australia, but it will give a great asset to Australia and the addition of a valuable unit of additional population.

Yours sincerely

81. *Herald* (Melbourne), 18 January 1939

Aborigines from various parts of Melbourne, and elsewhere, will take part in a pilgrimage to the grave of John Batman ... on Sunday, January 28, the day set apart for the observance of Aboriginal Sunday in Churches throughout the Commonwealth.

The pilgrimage is to mark the centenary of Batman's death, which took place on May 6, 1839, and the object of arranging for the presence of the aborigines is to emphasise the great respect in which the pioneer was held by the natives with whom he came in contact.

An address will be delivered by Mr Doug Nicholls, the well-known aboriginal footballer ...

Arrangements for the pilgrimage are being carried out by the Aborigines' Uplift Society, the Honorary Secretary of which is Mr A. P. A. Burdeu.

82. William Cooper, Secretary, Australian Aborigines' League, to the Prime Minister, Joseph Lyons, 4 February 1939

I am grateful to learn from Mr McEwen that the matter of our aboriginal race's future is coming up for discussion next week in Hobart. We have such a confidence in you and Mr McEwen that we are expecting that you are going to see full justice done to our people. Your attitude to the present has always impressed us and the Minister responsible for our destiny, the Minister for the Interior, has for some time and particularly with Mr McEwen and Mr Paterson, always impressed us with being solicitous for our welfare. We do feel, however, that it is consonant with British tradition that all people should have a say in their destiny. That is why we sought a member of Parliament and are asking that all Boards have Aboriginal representation and all aboriginal stations should allow the natives a share in the administration of their people.

Now that you have agreed, according to press notices, that there is to be a branch for Aboriginal Affairs under a suitable officer we would like to say that we have in mind one who would be very acceptable to natives, in the person of Dr T. G. H. Strehlow, now Patrol Officer for the Centre and located at Jay Creek reserve, near Alice Springs. Dr Strehlow was born and brought up among natives, the son of a man who did a monumental work for our people. In consonance with the principle of a voice in our own destiny we submit his name for your consideration as you come to the consideration of the matter. As you will know, Dr Strehlow has the requisite qualifications and in addition he has that love for the people he was brought up with that we feel he would be the one to implement the policy of the Administration.

Trusting that you may regard our claim to a voice in our own destiny as being in line with British policy,

I remain,

Yours sincerely and appreciatively

83. J. T. Patten, Secretary, Aborigines Progressive Association, and William Cooper, Secretary, Australian Aborigines' League, telegram to newspapers, 6 February 1939

Aboriginal men and women and children have left Cumeroogunga reservation for Victoria, due to intimidation, victimisation and starvation. Urgently needing food. Demand immediate inquiry.

84. William Cooper, Secretary, Australian Aborigines' League, to the Premier, New South Wales, Bertram Stevens, 20 February 1939

On November 28th I forwarded a letter, copy herewith, to the Chairman of the Board for the Protection of Aborigines, covering a petition of the natives of Cumeroogunga for the removal of Mr and Mrs M'Quiggan from the charge of the aboriginal station. To this communication I did not receive a reply but it was received for the names of the petitioners were posted at the Station, inviting those who wished to remove their names to do so. I submit that this is not in accordance with British tradition and would not be done for a fully white community and in itself constitutes a further grievance. The conditions which were so objectionable became more aggravated until the victimisation experienced forced a number of the people to leave New South Wales for Victoria, where they are living under very hard conditions.

I submitted our grievances and the people would have been satisfied if the enquiry had been granted, unless that enquiry was conducted by the very officers we are protesting about. We felt that in inviting the Chairman of the Board to arrange for this we were not going past those who had the administration of aboriginal affairs. Our people were prepared to submit their complaints and to support them with evidence and we felt that it was only necessary to do this when the will to do a fair thing would give some amelioration.

We aborigines are not agitators. We feel we have a right to British Fair Play and do make our representations in the right quarters, often with considerable satisfaction to ourselves, particularly in the Federal sphere. We ask only what we feel that the White public is willing to concede to us, for it is our experience that the general public is sympathetic to the Native cause. We feel we have grievances, not against the Government, nor so much against the Board itself as those who are employed by the Board and who act in a way the Board would not agree to, if it knew the facts. It never does know the facts for the only source of information by the Board is that submitted by the very officers we are protesting about. We are not an enemy people, and we are not in Nazi concentration camps. Why should we then be treated as though we were?

In regard to the present exodus from the station. This is our only way of protesting and of directing attention to the wrongs we are compelled to endure. It has had the effect of doing this and now that we have been able to bring the matter to the notice of the Government I trust we can expect that fair deal we seek. This is no ordinary strike, seeking conditions that employers will not concede. It is merely drawing attention to conditions which neither Government, Parliament nor Public would suffer, if they but knew them and to seek the conditions which we believe all three above mentioned would be glad to accede to.

A contented aboriginal population will be an asset, and we are satisfied very little, and we realise that the Government would like us to be happy and contented.

I have just visited the people in Barmah and the people tell me

1. That the treatment by the manager is very bad, that he uses vile language to them and is very abusive. The people are frightened of him at any time, for we have been cowed down so long, but the fact that he carries a rifle about with him makes matters worse. We have been decimated with the rifle among other things and fear the result of one being carried now. Because of his utter unsuitability they ask that he be removed from the superintendency.

2. The rations are inadequate. The scale will be well known to you and its value can be checked up on. Unemployed natives in Victoria receive the "dole" and we feel that unemployed natives should be nearer this scale than

they are. Our children are undernourished and this fact can be ascertained by examination.

3. Housing is inadequate and unsatisfactory.

4. The milk supply is impure and contaminated. With other factors the health of the people is bad and I append a list of infant deaths during the time Nurse Pratt was in charge of the treatment rooms. Mortality figures, including infant morality is too high and should be investigated.

5. Education at Cumeroogunga is most unsatisfactory and our children are not acquiring a reasonable education. We consider that the present teacher is unsuitable and should be replaced.

6. The people feel keenly that the women do not receive the Child endowment direct and do not have the spending of the money for their children which White mothers have. We particularly resent being refused endowment altogether since the trouble and would suggest that this matter be specially followed up. Is the action taken legal? Our people applied for the endowment on 6th and 13th inst. and were refused.

The setting out of the above facts will show that we feel that we labor under disabilities that should not have to be suffered. We trust we have satisfied you that an enquiry is justified. May we therefore ask that you make it possible for the people to return to their homes because if they do so under present conditions they know they will be subjected to worse treatment still than they have suffered in the past…

Yours sincerely

85. Workers' Voice, 1 March 1939, 'Half Caste Aborigine [Margaret Tucker], Conditions at Cummeroogunga'

"As a constant reader of the "Workers' Voice", and a half-caste aborigine who has experienced conditions at the Cummeroogunga Mission Station, I should like to confirm the article in your issue of February 11," writes "Half-caste Aborigine" to the "Voice".

"The conditions at Cummeroogunga are shocking. The rations issued by the administration are often rotten — not fit for pigs to eat. Housing and sanitary conditions are vile. Cows that supply the aborigine children with what little milk they receive drink at a damn in which sanitary Pans are washed. Some of these cows are tubercular, and should be destroyed. Giving evidence before a Commission in N.S.W., a former sister at the mission said that trachoma … is rampant in the settlement.

"The Mission has many acres of land which we could work up ourselves, but rather than give it to us the Aborigine 'Protection' Board leases it out for grazing purposes.

"Aboriginal men working on the Mission some years ago were 'given' blocks of densely timbered land. As soon as they had cleared the land it was taken away from them.

"The people at Cumeroogunga lived in constant fear of their children being taken from them by the Board, and being placed in homes. Wholesale kidnapping (it was nothing less) occurred on the Mission only a few years ago. The Manager sent the aboriginal men away on a rabbiting expedition.

"No sooner had they left the station than car loads of police (who had been waiting) dashed in and seized all the children they could get their hands on. These children were bundled into the cars and taken away for the Board to dispose of. Many of them never saw their parents again." [The seizure of aboriginal children by State authorities is still legal in New South Wales and Western Australia. — Ed.]

"These are only some of the terrible things that confront our People. I appeal to all 'Voice' readers to help us in our fight for liberty and freedom. Help us to protect ourselves from the clutches of the Aborigine Protection Board."

86. William Cooper, Secretary, Australian Aborigines' League, to the Minister for the Interior, John McEwen, Canberra, 19 April 1939

I was very distressed to read in the "Age" of 30th ultimo the following news from Canberra:

"One of the chief steps taken by the Department will aim to secure uniformity of Commonwealth aboriginal laws with those of West Australia, where the most modern legislation has been framed to date".

I do not regard all I read as being authentic for I am misreported myself but I would like to submit the following for your investigation:

1. While the legislation of West Australia is the latest it is the most reactionary in Australia, bringing my people into serfdom. Under this legislation a large number of regulations were promulgated and the whole of them have been disallowed by the West Australian Parliament. The Government, under pressure from Public opinion has agreed to bring in new legislation and then new regulations and is to call in the dissenting interests to confer in respect of the matter.

2. The man inspiring the legislation and framing the regulations is regarded by us and most aboriginal emancipatory organisations as the greatest enemy of our race. His policy of absorbtion of aborigines into the white population is as unfavorably viewed by us as by the white organisations. We prefer the administration of Mr Chinnery to Mr Neville.

May we therefore claim the investigation into the proposals by Mr Chinnery and the framing of suggested laws by the Federal Government. The announced policy of the Federal Government can be a basis for such legislation and we would suggest that the Government do in Federal matters what the West Australian government has agreed to do, viz: — consult missionary and ameliorative organisations including the Natives' own organisation. We will have pleasure in submitting a full policy for all classes and conditions of aborigines if you permit.

Thanking you for past interest and asking that we be assured of the same sympathetic treatment, helping us to become what we wish to be[:] "Australia's finest asset, the aborigines".

Yours sincerely

87. William Cooper, Secretary, Australian Aborigines' League, to the Premier, New South Wales, Bertram Stevens, 25 April 1939

At a meeting convened by this organisation but attended by a large number of the General Public, the following resolution has been carried, "That this meeting of Victorian Citizens strongly crities the Government of New South Wales for its failure to appoint an impartial enquiry into the just grievances of the aborigines of Cumeroogunga. It urges that an enquiry be immediately held and that Mr Mark Davidson, M.L.A. be appointed to conduct the enquiry".

In forwarding this resolution I would express disappointment in that our protests and requests in the matter have not resulted in more than an acknowledgement. No other State fails to respond to our correspondence, whatever their decision may be. In the Federal sphere the utmost courtesy and consideration is always shown and this we claim is consistent with the principles of British Justice which should be accorded to a persecuted minority.

May I have the Honor of a reply from you at an early date. The position at Cumeroogunga is now more acute for the Manager is intensifying the persecution we have had to bear in the past. It is now almost intolerable. If public opinion only knew the nature and extent of the persecution, victimisation, stoppage of rations, there would be a great outcry. If you knew yourself, it would stop at once.

Yours faithfully

88. *Argus*, 29 April 1939, 'Crossing the border: N.S.W. aborigines'

Aborigines from Cummeragunja Station (N.S.W.) are again crossing the border into Victoria as a protest against the treatment which they allege they are subject to.

Yesterday about 22 families moved into Victoria, according to reports received by the president of the Australian Aborigines League (Mr A. P. A. Burdeu). Others, he said last night, were moving across the border, and after the week-end there would be few of the 400 aborigines left on the station.

In February most of the aborigines crossed the border and remained in Victoria for about six weeks. The league persuaded them to return, pending the receipt of an answer to a request to the New South Wales Government for an inquiry into their charges.

The aborigines are now alleging, Mr Burdeu said, that those who crossed the border in February are being left out when rations are being distributed.

The league has sent a telegram to the Chief Secretary in New South Wales (Mr Bruxner), and to Mr Mark Davidson, M.L.A., who was chairman of the committee which inquired into the work of the Aborigines Board some years ago, informing them of the situation, and urging them to ensure an impartial distribution of rations, and to arrange for an inquiry at an early date.

The vice-chairman of the Victorian Aborigines Protection Board (Mr L. L. Chapman) said last night that, so long as the aborigines behaved themselves, no action would be taken against them by the Victorian authorities. They would not, however, be supplied with rations by the Victorian board.

89. *Herald* (Melbourne), 24 July 1939, 'Blacks refuse to go back: plight in camp'

Poorly dressed, short of blankets and protected from the rain and cold only by bag shelters, 44 natives are still camped on the Victorian side of the Murray near Barmah, determined not to return to Cumeroogunga (N.S.W.) Aboriginal Station until their complaints on conditions there have been properly investigated.

Included among the 44 are 18 children. During the week-end the river was only eight inches from the top of its banks, and flood waters threatened to add to their hardships.

Across on the Mooroopna side about 20 other natives are camped, also determined not to go back to Cumeroogunga under present conditions.

Inquiry Demand

The organising secretary of the Australian Aborigines' League (Mr G. Patten) said today that the natives were now entirely dependent on food and other help sent from Melbourne. They were not eligible for sustenance in Victoria and would get nothing from New South Wales while they remained across the river.

"They are suffering a lot of hardship but they would sooner do that and take a stand to force an inquiry, than go back to Cumeroogunga", Mr Patten said. "They feel that, if they return, there will be no hope of ever improving things for themselves or their children.

"Within a fortnight the league intends to launch a public campaign to draw attention to the condition of these and other natives in various settlements. People will be asked to sign a petition requesting the Federal Government to grant a Royal Commission to inquire into complaints.

"During the campaign we intend to tell the public something of what the Cumeroogunga natives have had to put up with."

90. The Fight at Cummeragunja (leaflet)

THE FIGHT AT CUMMERAGUNJA
Aborigines In Protest
Leave Government Supervised Camp
And Set Up STRIKE CAMP At
BARMAH — VICTORIA
(ON THE BANKS OF THE MURRAY)

Although supposedly reserved for the benefit of the aborigines, Cummerangunja's 3000 acres of fertile land, cleared by the aborigines, have been leased by the Government to squatters and pastoralists, with the exception of 60 acres, upon which are congested the 320 aborigines.

The 320 were forced to live in 35 two-roomed huts and four bag shelters.

Self-respect is undermined by "dole" living.

Starvation follows weekly rations, valued for adults at 3/5, for children 1/8 ?

Social, medical and educational services are insufficient and are so mal-ministered as to add to the general misery.

THE ABORIGINES' ASSISTANCE COMMITTEE
WORKING IN CONJUNCTION WITH THE NATIVES' ORGANISATION
THE AUSTRALIAN ABORIGINES' LEAGUE
Is Organising An Immediate Relief Of Distress
And The Creation Of Supporting Public Opinion
THE HELP OF YOUR MONEY WILL WIN THEIR FIGHT

91. A. P. A. Burdeu, President, Australian Aborigines' League, to the Chief Secretary, Victoria, 23 June 1939

Today Miss Ada Austin, quadroon black, was deemed ineligible for an old age pension for which she made application, due to the fact that she has a preponderance of aboriginal blood. The wrong suffered by aborigines, as there indicated has been brought to the notice of the Rt. Hon. the Prime Minister, asking to enact legislative amendments removing this blot on Australia's dealing with her natives. I believe that we will ultimately have success for we have been pressing for relief for years and believing that the Government does intend to do something. Meantime the poor woman, 62 years of age, till recently in domestic service but now feeling the weight of years and in poor health, saw me and in tears told me that she did not want to go back to the aboriginal camp to get the relief that she would there receive in rations as an aboriginal. She has Christian friends in Melbourne, where she is welcome to stay and where she will if she can get her ration issue in Melbourne. I mentioned this to the Secretary of the Board today but he assured me that the rations could only be available if she went back to Framlingham. Now I submit that if this is to be the practice, it should not be an inflexible rule and I feel that she, a single woman, could quite reasonably be exempted from the rule without it being claimed that an exception, granted for special reasons satisfactory to the Minister in charge of the Department, could be a precedent unless the circumstances were parallel and I cannot call to mind one old aboriginal woman who is, like Miss Austin, single.

I would urge that there is no cost involved. At Framlingham the police would issue the ration and the Aborigines' Uplift Society of which I am secretary, would, if desired, act without charge for the Department here, that is to say we would undertake delivery to her, thus saving trouble or cost to the Board.

It is very hard that she is refused the pension which morally is her right. It is doubly hard if she is to be forced back to an aboriginal status and from her friends to get the relief the State would give in those circumstances.

I make this definite request from the purely humanitarian standpoint and would request that no departmental practice be allowed to add to the hardship the unequal federal laws have forced on the woman.

Yours sincerely

92. William Cooper, Secretary, Australian Aborigines' League, to the Prime Minister, Robert Menzies, 5 October 1939

At the meeting of the League held last evening concern was expressed that the new Federal Policy for Aborigines, for which we have so long waited, was likely to have its implementation delayed, or at least curtailed, because of the need for all finance being made available for the prosecution of the war.

While we are most anxious, as our white fellow Australians are, to see the full resources of Australia marshalled for the prosecution of the war, we submit, that the last matter to suffer retrenchment is the good of the aboriginal cause, which is really a minority problem like, in some degree, the European matters which have caused the Empire to be at war. Those who are most needy and can suffer retrenchment less than any other portion of the population should not be called on only as a last resource.

May we have the honor of hearing that you will not permit of the implementation of our new deal being held up or delayed. Rather may we hope that all possible be done as soon as possible so that our suffering race may be more quickly brought to what is an aboriginal aspiration, viz: — "that the aboriginal problem be converted to the *ABORIGINAL ASSET* for the mutual good of White and Black in Australia".

With thanks,
Yours sincerely

93. William Cooper, Secretary, Australian Aborigines' League, to the Prime Minister, Robert Menzies, 5 October 1939

At a meeting of the league held last evening concern was felt at the fact that so many matters concerning aboriginal interests are either awaiting decision or have not yet reached that position. It was decided that you be asked to afford us the opportunity of meeting you as a deputation, when the following matters will be referred to: —

1. The petition to His Majesty, seeking representation in the Commonwealth Parliament for aborigines. As you will know, our Maori brothers have four members, including one minister of the Crown. Our request for one is, we feel, quite reasonable, more reasonable, we consider, that [i.e. than] representation should be afforded to the White population of the Northern Territory. Of course we understand that, if our request be granted, our member will not have a vote in matters before the House.

2. The New policy, "the Aboriginal Magna Carta", and its full implementation in the areas controlled by the Federal Parliament. Also the effect on the State Control of aborigines by the new policy. We have urged that the Federal Parliament should take over the State rights in this matter and we have been advised by certain State Administrations that they are not opposed to this.

3. Failing Federal control we have requested that a Federal Policy should be administered by the States, to be financed by the Federal Parliament on a percapita basis of the white population in the different States.

4. That provision be made for aborigines being qualified to receive community rights as Old Age and Invalid pensions, Maternity bonus and Franchise. At present aborigines are debarred from receiving what are rights of people of alien blood who are born in the land. Two men known by repute to you, but merely typical of others, who suffer this disability are David Uniapon and Douglas Nicholls. Aborigines whose income is within the range of taxability pay Income Tax and all other taxation.

Trusting that you will make it possible for us to meet you in deputation,
I remain,
Yours sincerely

94. William Cooper, Hon. Secretary, Australian Aborigines' League, circular letter, 24 November 1939

The sad condition of aborigines in Australia, differing in degree in each state, shows no marked improvement anywhere though amending legislation concerning our people has been effected or is contemplated in most States. The fact that no legislation ever improves our lot leads me to present what I consider the most likely way of effecting improvement, and I would request, in the name of the Aboriginal population, that you give consideration to this aspect, not by any means new, of course, and actually being in the policy of every organization working for better conditions for aborigines.

To every request for help or plea for better conditions comes back the cry, "There is no money", and, when it is remembered that Aborigines interests are a State matter and the States with the largest aboriginal population have the smallest white population, the statement seems reasonable. If, however, aboriginal interests are federalised, the whole population would bear the expense of aboriginal administration on a per capita basis. Beside this, the Federal Government has the new Federal policy for aborigines and are pledged to put it into operation.

We therefore request that you afford your support to our plea for Federal control under the new Federal policy and we would request that you write the Rt. Hon. The Prime Minister and the Hon. The Premier of your State indicating your support. We would also like to be advised of your decision in due course.

Yours Sincerely

95. *Argus*, 27 November 1939, '"Outcast in our own Land": Status of Aborigines'

"The skeleton in the cupboard of Australia's national life is its treatment of the aborigines," said Mr Doug Nicholls, the aborigine footballer, in an address at the Wesley Pleasant Sunday Afternoon service yesterday.

"We aborigines have not had a fair deal," he declared. "it was bad enough for us to lose our country, but it is one of the saddest stories of modern times that we should have become an outcast in our own land, with not even the rights and privileges that are extended to many aliens.

"We appeal for the right of education, for at least some of the rights of citizenship, for the chance to become useful citizens in the land that was ours by birth."

96. William Cooper, Secretary, Australian Aborigines' League, to the Prime Minister, Robert Menzies, 3 December 1939

The following matters addressed to you are again brought to your notice and I would request that they be finalised as soon as possible and you advise the position at present: —

1. Letter of 8th Sept. 1939 re the rights of aborigines who have reached a civilised status to full community rights as Old Age and Invalid pensions, maternity bonus and franchise.

2. Asking that no delay be permitted in respect of the new deal: That the finance for its implementation be made available in the full volume intended and as soon as possible.

3. Re our petition to his Majesty, asking inter alia, for representation in Parliament.

4. Asking that you receive a deputation from the league seeking a reply to four representations.

The whole of this correspondence and our other representations would be fully met if you were to pass amending legislation granting *full rights to aborigines who have attained civilised status*. We submit that a short bill could cover this and its passage would be quick. Failing this, we submit that it may be possible to do this by regulation under the War Precautions Act or its equivalent.

May we emphasise that this war is by reason of the tyranny over minorities and their cruel discriminating treatment. Australia cannot fight that cause in honesty while still oppressing her minority though we know that no white person sees this. Taking the matter of the last reported case of cruelty, that of refusing Miss [Ada] Austin, a charming, cultured, civilised aboriginal woman of Victoria a pension. Can a failure to rectify such a matter and allowing other such cases to occur be reconciled with British Justice.

Our treasurer, Doug Nicholls, broadcast over Wesley's pleasant Sunday Afternoon last week. His manuscript was submitted to the Censor, who disallowed certain portions, because it was not in the interests of Australia that the statements made, wholly concerning the utterance of white men and leaders in the White realm, should be given over the air to be picked up by enemy propagandists. Our community is so loyal that Doug gladly acquiesced.

This means that we may not broadcast our treatment but must just suffer it.

May I request that you close this whole matter by according to approved natives the full rights of white citizens *AND THOSE RIGHTS WHICH ARE THE PRIVILEGE OF ALIENS BORN IN THE LAND.*

The last war gave British Women their rights. May this one give the same to aborigines. Mr Lyons' government produced our MAGNA CARTA in the New policy. We do trust that your government will take the logical final steps for the outcome of the Federal policy must be the civilisation of the race who thus must ultimately come to a full Australian status.

The matter is urgent to us, some hungry mouths are still hungrier. Get rid of the disabilities and so link the aboriginal people in the more affectionate loyalty to the Empire.

We request your personal dealing with this matter.

Yours sincerely

97. William Cooper to Mrs W. A. Norman, 30 July 1940

Your very kind and sincere letter, dated 22nd inst., reached me this morning and without doubt I must say that I cannot find enough happy words to express my deep appreciation for this letter I have received from you; especially where you speak of your dear beloved father and mother, and of dear Maloga.[61] I often cast my mind back to them, and the dear old place, and at times it brings tears in my eyes when thinking of the glorious hours, days and months, we spent together; the beautiful singing, the picnics, the games. — Your father's voice still rings in my ears: We never ever had singing like we did at Maloga.

When we left Maloga, it appeared to me as though we left Paradise. After this we were at Cumeroogunga, for about four years, when the people became wrecked. Our people never were the same after they left Maloga: they steadily drifted back, almost to where they started from.

On account of the cruel administration which our people had to suffer, I was obliged to leave Cumeroogunga. I have been away from Cumeroogunga for over 30 years.

I came here in the year 1931 and have been here ever since. During all this time I have been pleading for my people throughout Australia, and only, after working for seven years, I got slight results in the Northern Territory. South Australia is now also improving, but Queensland, with the exception of Cowal Creek, where an Aboriginal leader, Jomen Tamwoy, has gathered together three tribes, taught them about God and they have now, without outside assistance, built their own little homes with gardens in front. They are over 150 persons, they grow their own vegetables and as there are plenty of wild cattle, they are not short of meat. As far as the Government is concerned, Queensland is at a standstill. In W.A. and N.S.W. natives are still very badly treated.

You know that there is much to be done before the Abo can be parallel with the white man. The Government is very unjust and stubborn; for it will not do anything for our people if it can avoid it, for they have often promised in reply to my letters, but that is about as far as they have got so far: however; we must continue asking God to help to pull us through our struggle for justice.

It will be news to you to hear of my brothers and sisters. You will be sorry to hear that Edgar, Lizzie, Johnny, and Aaron have passed away[,] Jack and Bobby Cooper, and Mrs James, and Myself are all well. I don't know if you will remember all I have mentioned, for you were a very little girl when you were at Maloga. You never told me about your sister and brothers! Are any of them in Melbourne? Let me know when you write again, please.

I am enclosing you a subscription list; it is to help the League forward. I will be glad if you will head the list, and if, in your position, you can get other sympathetic friends to help me. I am trying very ernestly to raise enough money to hire the Melbourne Town Hall for a big public meeting. We must make our voices heard, but I feel sure that such a meeting would do a lot of good. I trust you will not think that I am asking too much. I do so because I feel you have our interest at heart. I have gained an amount of public sympathy, but the Governments keep neglecting all requests. I am still fighting on, and though disheartened at times, I know God sees all, and that if we keep on trusting Him, He WILL see that we get justice, and so I keep on going, and shall do so till the end.

Your sincere friend

98. William Cooper to Mrs W. A. Norman, 21 August 1940

Your letter dated 4.8.40 reached me safely last night.

I am very pleased to note how interested you are in our natives and the question[s] you have asked me have really created great joy in me. You are the first one to ask so many important questions concerning our aborigines and I have much pleasure in answering: —

1. We are earnestly pleading for Federal Control as it is almost impossible to be granted an aboriginal representative in Parliament while natives are under State control. It is therefore the duty of every person to persuade the authorities to grant Federal Control.

2. The uncivilised natives should remain as they are at present but should be well protected by the various governments from harm. They should be assured of sufficient food when drought or other circumstances limit their natural supply.

3. The Semi-civilised should be brought under Christian control and educated to take their place in the community.

4. Civilised natives who are capable should be compensated with land out of the countless millions of acres taken from them. They should be helped to cultivate this land for their own benefit.

5. Large settlements like Cumeroogunga can definitely be governed by the natives themselves and not be supervised at the beck and call of a white man. As you know, many of the natives know more than many of the managers of Government stations, who are often not the best type of men to be placed in charge of these stations.

6. I will be 80 years of age on 18th December next and I feel that I would be unable to represent my people in Parliament. I am sorry to say that I do not know of one aboriginal in Australia that I could recommend for the job.

In conclusion I would like to say that we have strong support from the people of Melbourne, but, on account of the war we are unable to make appeals to carry on our work. We are therefore grateful for what our friends donate to us to help us on. You will be surprised to hear that I have been working for the cause for nine years without any payment and have spent over £100 of my own money and I am only drawing a pension. However I don't mind for it is for a good cause and I have European blood in my veins. I am endeavouring to clear myself with the Supreme Ruler from the cruelty that is being committed against the original occupants of this country. I am living in hopes of being rewarded in the end

I feel sure that you will agree with me when I say that the vast majority of Church people in Australia are not living up to their profession when they allow such cruelty and neglect to continue. I am not driving at any individual but the people as a whole.

It was very unfortunate for the aborigines to lose your dearly beloved father and mother. Had they lived and worked to now we would have had aboriginal Doctors, Lawyers, Mechanical Engineers and other professional people and would also have had educated natives capable of representing our people in Parliament. Unfortunately the loss of your dear father has prolonged the Uplift of the natives.

Before closing I wish to ask if you can find the Queen's proclamation for the protection of the aborigines. Dad had one copy when you were at Maloga. It would be great use to me if I could get it.

I will now close with kindest regards,

I am, your sincere friend

99. William Cooper, Secretary, Australian Aborigines' League, to the Prime Minister, Robert Menzies, 31 August 1940

In your letter of May 1939 and on other occasions you have expressed your "active interest in the welfare of the Australian Aborigines" and I am therefore again writing to bring the needs of my people to your notice before the Federal Elections.

I regret troubling you when the gravity of the International situation is needing your constant attention but I would point to the fact that the serious condition of my people does call for immediate consideration. Unless their position is speedily rectified their condition will inevitably deteriorate, therefore from the point of view of economy alone it is surely wise to increase financial assistance and so help them to become useful members of the community instead of the outcasts they must otherwise become.

Are you in favour of carrying out the Federal Governments policy as outlined by Mr McEwen when Minister for the Interior, or at least the main essentials of this policy as recommended by Mr Chinnery, Director of Native Affairs?

These are —

1. The provision of more reserves for the preservation of the natives still in their tribal state of culture.

2. The provision of Mission or Government Stations on the fringe of the reserves for the establishment of pastoral and other industries. This would prevent the drift to the towns which is bringing about the deterioration and inevitable extinction of my people. Land for their own use is the first essential for my people and any that is given now is small compensation for all they have lost.

3. We also desire the appointment of more District and Patrol Officers with Assistant Patrol officers of aboriginal blood instead of native police who will administer justice, render medical assistance and supply rations where necessary.

You will realise that for carrying out this policy an adequate financial grant is essential.

We congratulate the Federal Government on the appointment of Mr Chinnery as Director of Native Affairs in the Northern Territory but would point out the fallacy of expecting him to carry out his work effectively unless the Government places the means at his disposal. If the Government refuses to go forward because of the war it will find that after the war it will be too late for any real constructive work for my people.

We would point to the deplorable moral conditions which exist at present in Darwin owing to the large number of troops, and to the number of undesirable civilians who have flocked to the town and we request you to take immediate steps to remedy this state of affairs. We ask you to press for the provision of several trained Women Protectors, to be assisted by women protectors of aboriginal blood, for the proper protection of aboriginal and halfcaste women. We commend the steps already taken by Mr Chinnery for improved educational and recreational facilities and urge that still greater steps be taken in this direction at a centre further removed from Darwin than the present compound.

My League is pressing for the federalisation of aboriginal affairs with a national policy of a constructive character, but until this can be brought about we would urge the Federal Government to provide a grant to Western Australia for the purpose of aboriginal education. W.A. has the largest aboriginal and smallest white population of all mainland states and therefore cannot, or will not, adequately tackle this problem. Half-castes in the S.W. of W.A. are growing up in deplorable squalor and are becoming a community of out-castes. Out of 1,600 children in the S.W. less than one quarter are receiving any education.

If Australia is sincere in her stand for democracy and her desire to free the peoples of other lands from the oppression of Hitlerism, her sincerity will be shown by the attitude she adopts towards her own exploited minority. Lip service to democracy and Christianity is not enough. "By their fruits ye shall know them".

I would point to the fact that no answer has been given to the petition of my League for an aboriginal representative in Parliament.

Trusting you will find time to deal with this important matter.

Yours faithfully ...

P.S. I hope to attend your meeting in the Camberwell Town Hall on Monday evening.

100. *Sun* (Melbourne), November 1940, '"White people must think black": Aboriginal spokesman's eloquent plea for his people'

Australians were raving about persecuted minorities in other parts of the world, but were they ready to voice their support for the unjustly treated aboriginal minority in Australia? Mr Doug Nicholls, aboriginal preacher, and former League footballer, asked the question at the Unitarian Church yesterday.

"We want to say good-bye to compounds and native reserves," he said. "We want to live in co-operation, to help as Australia progresses.

"I saw my people on the Nullabor Plain when I was crossing by train, running to and fro by the carriages, begging for food, crying "Gibbit, gibbit".

"They seized pieces of apple peel, scraps of bread that were thrown out the windows and doors. I can never forget it.

"White people must learn to think black"

"When you took this land from us you took us with it. We are your responsibility.

"Although we try to live as good citizens and pay our taxes, we are denied all the privileges of nationhood. We cannot vote. In New South Wales our children cannot go beyond the third grade in school.

"The authorities may close the schools to them; but they cannot close the schools of human experience."

Aborigines capable of expressing themselves on current matters cannot reasonably be treated as stone age people. This is what our administration is doing.

Notes

1. See Mavis Thorpe Clark, *Pastor Doug: The Story of Sir Douglas Nicholls, Aboriginal Leader*, Lansdowne Press, Melbourne, 1965, chapter 9.
2. See Diane Barwick, 'A Little More than Kin': Regional Affiliation and Group Identity Among Aboriginal Migrants in Melbourne, PhD, Australian National University, 1963; and Andrew Markus, *Governing Savages*, Allen & Unwin, Sydney, 1990. Markus's selection of Cooper's letters, *Blood from a Stone: William Cooper and the Australian Aborigines' League*, first published in 1986 by Monash Publications in History, consisted of fifty-three documents; a revised edition, published by Allen & Unwin in 1988, had more illustrative material and an extra document.
3. Jack Horner, *Vote Ferguson for Aboriginal Freedom: A Biography*, Australian and New Zealand Book Company, Sydney, 1974; Barwick, 'William Cooper', *Australian Dictionary of Biography*, vol. 8, 1890–1939, Melbourne University Press, Melbourne, 1981, pp. 107–08; Andrew Markus, 'William Cooper and the 1937 Petition to the King', *Aboriginal History*, vol. 7, pt 1, 1983, pp. 46–60; Horner & Marcia Langton, 'The Day of Mourning', in Bill Gammage & Peter Spearritt (eds), *Australians 1938*, Fairfax Syme & Weldon, Sydney, 1987, pp. 29–35; Markus, *Governing Savages*, pp. 183–89; Russell McGregor, 'Protest and Progress: Aboriginal Activism in the 1930s', *Australian Historical Studies*, vol. 25, no. 101, 1993, pp. 555–68; Heather Goodall, *Invasion to Embassy: Land in Aboriginal Politics in New South Wales, 1770–1972*, Black Books/Allen & Unwin, Sydney, 1996, pp. 78–79, 185–92, 230–32, 247–50; Geoff Stokes, 'Citizenship and Aboriginality: Two Conceptions of Identity in Aboriginal Political Thought', in Stokes (ed.), *The Politics of Identity in Australia*, Cambridge University Press, Melbourne, 1997, pp. 158–71; The most recent discussion of Cooper's work appears in Bain Attwood, *Rights for Aborigines*, Allen & Unwin, Sydney, 2003, chapters 2 & 3.
4. This account of Cooper's life draws on the following sources: 'Episodes of Interest in the Life of the Late William Cooper (Told by Himself)', Norman Papers, State Library of South Australia, PRG 422; William Cooper to E. R. B. Gribble, 16 July 1933, E. R. B. Gribble Papers, AIATSIS, MS 1515/11; Helen Baillie to A. P. Elkin, 11 June [1934], A. P. Elkin Papers, University of Sydney Archives, series 1/12/124; **27, 43, 53**; Barwick, 'William Cooper', p. 107.
5. Daniel Matthews, Diary, 6 August 1874, cited Nancy Cato, *Mister Maloga: Daniel Matthews and his Mission, Murray River, 1864–1902*, University of Queensland Press, St Lucia, 1976, p. 69; Matthews, Diary, 1876, cited Cato, *Mister Maloga*, p. 80.
6. Cooper spelled the name of this reserve in different ways: Cumeroogunja, Cumerogunja and, most commonly, Cumeroogunga.

7   Matthews, Diary, 1884, cited Cato, *Mister Maloga*, p. 167.
8   Baillie to Elkin, 11 June [1934].
9   A. P. A. Burdeu to William Morley, 2 July 1939, APNR Papers, University of Sydney Archives, series 7; Baillie to Elkin, 11 June [1934].
10 Cooper himself claimed that he went to Melbourne in 1931 (**97**) but there is no other evidence this is so.
11 Clark, *Pastor Doug*, pp. 87–88.
12 See Diane Barwick, *Rebellion at Coranderrk*, Aboriginal History Inc, Canberra, 1998.
13 Matthews, letters to the editor, *Riverine Herald*, 1866, *Bendigo Advertiser*, 21 August 1874, cited Cato, *Mister Maloga*, pp. 28, 53.
14 Cato, *Mister Maloga*, p. 347.
15 Cooper, 'Victory', undated, Norman Papers.
16 McGregor, 'Protest and Progress', p. 567.
17 *Sydney Morning Herald*, 15 November 1927.
18 Goodall, *Invasion to Embassy*, p. 103.
19 ibid. Goodall points out that Joe Anderson, in calling for a petition, 'stated that Aborigines had "kings in their own right", long before white men came to Australia'. She also contends that Anderson used the title 'King Burraga' as a means of 'insisting on an acknowledgment of the equality of status between Aboriginal and English spokespeople or figureheads' (A History of Aboriginal Communities in New South Wales, 1909–1939, PhD, University of Sydney, 1982, p. 252). Anderson's comment appears in **12**.
20 Baillie to Elkin, 11 June [1934]; see John A. Williams, *Politics of the New Zealand Maori: Protest and Cooperation, 1891–1909*, Auckland University Press, Auckland, 1969, chapter 4.
21 William Cooper to the Victorian Board for the Protection of Aborigines, September [1933], NAA, B337, item 187.
22 *Australian Abo Call*, no. 1, 1938.
23 In a letter written in 1938 Cooper also referred to 'adding a new province to Australia' (**72**).
24 Petition, House of Representatives, *Votes and Proceedings*, 1926–28, vol. 1, pp. 691–94; Aborigines Protection League, The Proposed Aboriginal State Manifesto, NAA, A1/1, 1932/4262. See Michael Roe, 'A Model Aboriginal State', *Aboriginal History*, vol. 10, pt 1, 1986, pp. 40–44; Markus, *Governing Savages*, pp. 168–72; Kevin Blackburn, 'White Agitation for an Aboriginal State in Australia (1925–1929)', *Australian Journal of Politics and History*, vol. 45, no. 2, 1999, pp. 157–80.
25 Burdeu to Mrs W. A. Norman, 23 September 1940, Norman Papers.
26 See Attwood, *Rights for Aborigines*, chapter 4.
27 Baillie, 'Some Recollections of Mr A. P. A. Burdeu', Elkin Papers, 1/12/134; Clark, *Pastor Doug*, p. 87.
28 Cooper to W. G. Sprigg, 22 February 1936, Women's International League of Peace and Freedom Papers, State Library of Victoria, MS 9377/1726/1; AAL, Annual Report, 1936, SRNSW, 12/8749B.

29   Burdeu to Sir John Harris, 11 March 1936, ASS Papers, Rhodes House Library, Oxford, series 22, G378; Burdeu to Ruth Swann, 18 April 1940, APNR Papers, series 7; Burdeu to Norman, 23 September 1940; Burdeu to Elkin, 2 July 1941, Elkin Papers, 1/12/134; Baillie, 'Some Recollections'. Burdeu's work for the League was shaped by his keen awareness that Aborigines' aspirations were 'completely different from the white man's outlook'. This in turn can be attributed to his familiarity with the Aboriginal community in Melbourne. Burdeu believed he had a special, even unique relationship 'to the aboriginal problem'; he had, he asserted, come 'to the work with a knowledge of the heartthrobs of the people'. This experience had enabled him to 'see the problem through Aboriginal eyes'—'I meet natives in the[ir] own homes and know their inner lives'—and this had given him 'another point of view'. Burdeu might have exaggerated his degree of insight. Bill Ferguson, for example, was highly critical of him, claiming there was 'no such thing as a white man who can think black' and complaining that Burdeu had 'disorganised the Aborigines of Victoria altogether'. Yet, there is little doubt that Burdeu was much liked by Aboriginal people in Melbourne and was regarded as kin. Helen Baillie reckoned he had become their 'firm friend and councillor', and observed that he 'had a wonderful memory for all the dark folk', would always ask after the various members of a family by name, and was 'affectionately known as "Pop"' (Burdeu to Elkin, 2 July 1941; Baillie, 'Some Recollections'; William Ferguson to Elkin, 18 December 1941, Elkin Papers, 1/12/131).

30   Baillie to Elkin, 11 June [1934]; Burdeu to Premier, NSW, 7 August 1939, SRNSW, 12/8749B; Burdeu to Norman, 23 September 1940.

31   See Leanne Reinke, Community, Communication and Contradiction: The Political Implications of Changing Modes of Communication in Indigenous Communities of Australia and Mexico, PhD, Monash University, 2001, pp. 104, 119–20.

32   McGregor, 'Protest and Progress', p. 555.

33   For example, Margaret Tucker, Doug Nicholls, Caleb Morgan, Lynch Cooper and Hylus Briggs.

34   Goodall, *Invasion to Embassy*, pp. 102–03.

35   'Episodes of Interest'.

36   Amy Brown to Morley, 30 June 1938, Elkin Papers, 12/68/147; Donald Thomson, 'Aboriginal Fallacies Exploded', *Herald*, 16 May 1938; Tom Wright to the editor, the *Advocate*, 25 October 1939, Tom and Mary Wright Papers, Noel Butlin Archives Centre, Australian National University, MS Z267/8; Cooper to John McEwen, From an Educated Aboriginal, 21 January 1939, NAA, A659, 1940/1/858.

37   See document 34 in Markus, *Blood from a Stone*, Allen & Unwin, Sydney, 1988, pp. 78–79.

38   Chief Protector of Aborigines, South Australia, to Secretary, Victorian Board for the Protection of Aborigines, 4 June 1936, PROVic, 3992P/2557/L3734.

39   Sadly, it seems the petition was later destroyed. Certainly, the National Archives of Australia have never been able to find it in their collections.

40   A day of this nature seems to have been first suggested by humanitarians at a conference of government, missionary and other organisations in 1929, which Shadrach James attended (Report of Conference of Representatives of Missions, Societies, and Associations…12 April 1929, NAA, A1, 1933/8782).

41 For example, Selby had written a history of Victoria in 1924 in which he had made several references to the treaty; he had performed historical pageants in 1934 that included a scene featuring the signing of the treaty; and he had organised an event in 1935 commemorating the hundredth anniversary of the treaty (*The Old Pioneers' Memorial History of Melbourne*, Old Pioneers' Memorial Fund, Melbourne, [1924], pp. 24–25, 35, 38). Handbill and an advertisement for pageants, Isaac Selby Papers, Royal Historical Society of Victoria, MS 694; *Age*, 30 May 1935.

42 Souvenir Programme: Grand Pioneer Rally and Historical Service at the Spot Where Batman Found the Yarra, 24 January 1937, Selby Papers.

43 ibid. For correspondence regarding the concert, see Selby Papers; for a discussion of the concert, see Attwood, *Rights for Aborigines*, pp. 72–73.

44 McEwen, submission to Cabinet, Australian Aborigines' League—Petition to His Majesty the King', 1 February 1938, NAA, A461, A300/1, Pt III, reproduced in Markus, 'William Cooper', p. 58.

45 Cooper and Burdeu added to this statement in January 1939 and forwarded it to the Minister for the Interior, John McEwen (From an Educated Aboriginal).

46 In December 2002 the Jewish Holocaust Museum and Research Centre in Melbourne unveiled a plaque acknowledging this action (*Australian Jewish News*, 13 December 2002).

47 See Goodall, *Invasion to Embassy*, p. 192.

48 Morley to G. C. Gollan, 15 March 1939, APNR Papers, series 7.

49 For accounts of the walk-off, see Goodall, *Invasion to Embassy*, chapter 18, and Attwood, *Rights for Aborigines*, pp. 45–53.

50 See Theresa Clements, *From Old Maloga: The Memoirs of an Aboriginal Woman*, Fraser & Morphet, Prahran, no date, p. 8; Horner, *Vote Ferguson*, p. 79; Alick Jackomos and Derek Fowell (comps), *Living Aboriginal History of Victoria: Stories in the Oral Tradition*, Cambridge University Press, Melbourne, 1991, pp. 180, 182, 186.

51 McEwen to Burdeu, 17 March 1938, and Jack Patten to Joseph Lyons, 9 December 1938, NAA, B1535, 929/19/912; Robert A. Hall, *The Black Diggers: Aborigines and Torres Strait Islanders in the Second World War* (1989), Aboriginal Studies Press, Canberra, 1997, p. 8.

52 See Hall, *Black Diggers*, pp. 13–26.

53 Burdeu to the Secretary to the Prime Minister, 30 March 1941, MP508/1, 275/750/1310; William Onus to John Curtin, 30 June 1941, South Australian State Archives, SRG 250/41, cited Hall, *Black Diggers*, p. 22. Cooper also said this: 'They were wanted to fight to make Australia safe for those who took it from the Natives' ('Episodes of Interest').

54. Clark, *Pastor Doug*, p. 90; *Victorian Aborigines Advancement League Newsletter*, no. 17, 1969, p. 3, no. 19, 1969, p. 8; Wayne Atkinson, '"Not One Iota" of Land Justice: Reflections on the Yorta Yorta Native Title Claim 1994–2001', *Indigenous Law Bulletin*, vol. 5, no. 6, 2001, p. 23.

55 Herbert Basedow was a South Australia anthropologist and member of parliament, and the author of *The Australian Aboriginal* (1925). In 1911 he was Chief Protector of Aborigines for the Northern Territory very briefly and later was a member of the Aborigines Protection League.

56 Donald Thomson, 'A Plea for the Vanishing Race', *Herald*, 22 March 1930. Drawing on his recent fieldwork in the Cape York Peninsula, Thomson highlighted what he saw as the positive attributes of Aborigines, such as the 'loyalty

and courage and selfless devotion of which the blackfellow is capable in serving the white man', and argued that extinction of the Aborigines in the near future could only be prevented by 'complete change of policy on our part'. The only hope lay in 'complete segregation in adequate reserves'.

57   Sir Walter Baldwin Spencer, Professor of Biology at the University of Melbourne, was Australia's leading anthropologist in the late nineteenth and early twentieth centuries, the co-author of *Native Tribes of Central Australia* (1899) and *Across Australia* (1912), and the author of *Wanderings in Wild Australia* (1929).

58   On 29 March 1935 the Melbourne *Herald* carried an article under the heading 'Fantastic Stories of Our Cruelty to Blacks' which reported publicity accorded to the views of an English writer, Mr S. Morrell, in his homeland and in Sweden. Morrell asserted that Aborigines in the north were denied justice in courts of law; that a missionary who reported a massacre of Aborigines by police was removed while the police were exonerated; that Aborigines were robbed of their land; that for the sum of ten shillings a settler could buy a licence 'which gives him power to use the labor of natives without any other cost'; that Aboriginal women were thrashed and otherwise mistreated; that 'until recently it was the usual Sunday sport among white settlers to go out and hunt natives with guns'.

59   The letter was published in the *Herald*, 22 February 1937, under the heading 'APPEAL FOR ABORIGINALS Equality with Whites Sought', with this preface:'Full "equality and responsibility" with whites is claimed by the Australian Aborigines' League'.

60   Much of this was incorporated in another document, 'From an Educated Aboriginal', which Cooper sent to John McEwen on 21 January 1939. This corrected typographical errors in 'From an Educated Black' and these emendations have been included in our transcription here.

61   The father and mother were Daniel and Janet Matthews.

Sources for documents

1 *Riverine Herald*, 20 July 1887

2 Colonial Secretary's Correspondence, 1/2667, SRNSW

9, 17 Board for the Protection of the Aborigines, Victoria, 'Aborigines Case Files: William Cooper', NAA, CRS B337, item 187

11, 21, 22, 32, 36, 65, 92, 93, 96 Prime Minister's Department, Correspondence files, 'Aboriginals ... Policy ... ', NAA, CRS A461, A300/1, pts II & III

12 Screensound (Melbourne)

13, 16, 18, 19, 20, 26, 27, 70 Department of the Interior, Correspondence files, 'Representation of Aborigines in the Commonwealth Parliament', NAA, CRS A431, 1949/1591

14, 15, 23, 28 E. R. B. Gribble Papers, AIATSIS, MS 1515/11

25 Department of the Interior, Correspondence files, 'Welfare of Aboriginals in the Northern Territory: Deputation to Minister, 23.1.35', NAA, CRS A1, 1935/3951

29, 41, 45, 57 Anti-Slavery Society Papers, Rhodes House, Oxford, series 22, G377, G378, G379

30, 39, 47, 48, 59, 74, 84, 87 Premier's Department, New South Wales, 'Treatment of Aboriginals in New South Wales, 1936–63', pt 1, 12/8749, A36/1028 & A38/931

31, 37, 44, 50, 51, 61, 63, 66, 69, 73, 77, 78, 80, 82, 86, 90, 99 Department of the Interior, Correspondence files, 'Australian Aborigines League', NAA, CRS A659, 1940/1/858

32 A. P. Elkin Papers, University of Sydney Archives, series 68/148

34 Department of the Interior, Correspondence files, 'Corroborees at Aboriginal Compound, Darwin', NAA, CRS A1, 1936/7014

33, 71, 94 APNR Papers, University of Sydney Archives, series 7

43, 46, 49 Isaac Selby Papers, Royal Historical Society of Victoria, MS 694/226

54 Attorney-General's Department, Correspondence files, 'Australian Aborigines' League, Petition to the King — Representation in the Commonwealth Parliament', NAA, CRS 432, 1937/1191

58 P. R. Stephensen Papers, Mitchell Library, State Library of New South Wales, MS 1284

83 *Daily News*, 7 February 1939

91 Chief Secretary's Office, Victoria, Correspondence files, PROVic, VPRS 3992/P, unit 2813, file R4932

97, 98 Mortlock Library, State Library of South Australia, PRG 422

Bibliography

Official sources

Archival

National Archives of Australia

Attorney-General's Department, Correspondence files, 'Australian Aborigines' League, Petition to the King — Representation in the Commonwealth Parliament', CRS 432, 1937/1191.

Board for the Protection of the Aborigines, Victoria, 'Aborigines Case Files: William Cooper', CRS B337, item 187.

Department of the Interior, Correspondence files, 'Aboriginal Welfare Conference — Melbourne — 1933', CRS A1, 1933/8782.

——, 'Australian Aborigines League', CRS A659, 1940/1/858.

——, 'Corroborees at Aboriginal Compound, Darwin', CRS A1, 1936/7014.

——, 'E. E. Kramer Abo. Affairs N.T.', CRS A1, 1936/12778.

——, 'Representation of Aborigines in the Commonwealth Parliament', CRS A431, 1949/1591.

——, 'Welfare of Aboriginals in the Northern Territory: Deputation to Minister, 23.1.35', CRS A1, 1935/3951.

Prime Minister's Department, Correspondence files, 'Aboriginals—Policy...', CRS A461, A300/1, pts II & III.

Public Record Office Victoria

Chief Secretary's Office, Victoria, Correspondence files, VPRS 3992.

State Records Office of Western Australia

Western Australia, Department of Native Affairs, 'Australian Aborigines' League', 75/1936.

State Records New South Wales

Aborigines Protection Board and Aborigines Welfare Board, Minutes, CGS 2
Colonial Secretary's Correspondence, 1/2667.

Premier's Department, New South Wales, 'Treatment of Aboriginals in New South Wales, 1936–63', pt 1, 12/8749, A36/1028 & A38/931.

State Records of South Australia

Chief Secretary's Department, Inwards Correspondence, GRG 52/1, 1936.

Printed

Census of the Commonwealth of Australia 30 June 1933.

Other sources

Manuscript

Anti-Slavery Society Papers, Rhodes House Library, Oxford, series 22.

Association for the Protection of Native Races Papers, University of Sydney Archives.

A. P. Elkin Papers, University of Sydney Archives.

E. R. B. Gribble Papers, AIATSIS, MS 1515.

Norman Papers, State Library of South Australia, PRG 422.

Isaac Selby Papers, Royal Historical Society of Victoria, MS 694.

P. R. Stephensen Papers, Mitchell Library, State Library of New South Wales, MS 1284.

Women's International League of Peace and Freedom Papers, State Library of Victoria, MS 9377.

A. W. R. Vroland Papers, National Library of Australia, MS 3991.

Tom and Mary Wright Papers, Noel Butlin Archives Centre, Australian National University, MS Z267.

Newspapers and periodicals

Age
Argus
Australian Abo Call
Australian Intercollegian
Daily News
Dawn
Herald (Melbourne)
Indigenous Law Bulletin
Labor Call
Ladder
Riverine Herald
Sun (Melbourne)
Uplift
Victorian Aborigines Advancement League Newsletter
West Australian
Woman Today
Workers' Voice

Secondary sources

Books, essays and articles

Attwood, Bain, *Rights for Aborigines*, Allen & Unwin, Sydney, 2003.

Attwood, Bain & Andrew Markus, *The Struggle for Aboriginal Rights: A Documentary History*, Allen & Unwin, Sydney, 1999.

Barwick, Diane, 'Aunty Ellen: The Pastor's Wife', in Isabel White et al. (eds), *Fighters and Singers: The Lives of Some Australian Aboriginal Women*, Allen & Unwin, Sydney,

1985, pp. 175–99.

——, 'Coranderrk and Cumeroogunga: Pioneers and Policy', in T. Scarlett Epstein and David H. Penny (eds), *Opportunity and Response: Case Studies in Economic Development*, C. Hurst, London, 1972, pp. 11–68.

——, *Rebellion at Coranderrk*, Aboriginal History Inc., Canberra, 1998.

——, 'William Cooper', *Australian Dictionary of Biography*, vol. 8, 1890–1939, Melbourne University Press, Melbourne, 1981, pp. 107–08.

Blackburn, Kevin, 'White Agitation for an Aboriginal State in Australia (1925–1929)', *Australian Journal of Politics and History*, vol. 45, no. 2, 1999, pp. 157–80.

Bowe, Heather et al., *Yorta Yorta Language Heritage*, Department of Linguistics, Monash University, 1997.

Cato, Nancy, *Mister Maloga: Daniel Matthews and His Mission, Murray River, 1864–1902*, University of Queensland Press, St Lucia, 1976.

Clark, Mavis Thorpe, *Pastor Doug: The Story of Sir Douglas Nicholls, Aboriginal Leader*, Lansdowne Press, Melbourne, 1965.

Clements, Theresa, *From Old Maloga: The Memoirs of an Aboriginal Woman*, Fraser & Morphet, Prahran, no date.

Goodall, Heather, *Invasion to Embassy: Land in Aboriginal Politics in New South Wales, 1770–1972*, Black Books/Allen & Unwin, Sydney, 1996.

Haebich, Anna, *For Their Own Good: Aborigines and Government in the Southwest of Western Australia, 1900–1940*, University of Western Australian Press, Nedlands, 1988.

Hall, Robert A., *The Black Diggers: Aborigines and Torres Strait Islanders in the Second World War* (1989), Aboriginal Studies Press, Canberra, 1997.

Horner, Jack, *Vote Ferguson for Aboriginal Freedom: A Biography*, Australian and New Zealand Book Company, Sydney, 1974.

Horner, Jack & Marcia Langton, 'The Day of Mourning', in Bill Gammage & Peter Spearritt (eds), *Australians 1938*, Fairfax Syme & Weldon, Sydney, 1987, pp. 29–35.

Jackomos, Alick & Derek Fowell, *Living Aboriginal History of Victoria: Stories in the Oral Tradition*, Cambridge University Press, Melbourne, 1991.

Lake, Marilyn, *Getting Equal: The History of Australian Feminism*, Allen & Unwin, Sydney, 1999.

McGregor, Russell, *Imagined Destinies: Aboriginal Australians and the Doomed Race Theory, 1880–1939*, Melbourne University Press, Melbourne, 1997.

——, 'Protest and Progress: Aboriginal Activism in the 1930s', *Australian Historical Studies*, vol. 25, no. 101, 1993, pp. 555–68.

Markus, Andrew, 'After the Outward Appearance: Scientists, Administrators and Politicians', in Bill Gammage & Andrew Markus (eds), *All That Dirt: Aborigines 1938*, History Project Inc., Canberra, 1982, pp. 83–106.

——, *Blood From a Stone: William Cooper and the Australian Aborigines' League*, Allen & Unwin, Sydney, 1988.

——, *Governing Savages*, Allen & Unwin, Sydney, 1990.

——, 'William Cooper and the 1937 Petition to the King', *Aboriginal History*, vol. 7, pt 1, 1983, pp. 46–60.

Maynard, John, 'Vision, Voice and Influence: The Rise of the Australian Aboriginal Progressive Association', *Australian Historical Studies*, vol. 34, no. 11, 2003, pp. 91–105.

Paisley, Fiona, *Loving Protection?: Australian Feminism and Aboriginal Women's Rights 1919–1939*, Melbourne University Press, Melbourne, 2000.

Read, Peter, *A Hundred Years War: The Wiradjuri People and the State*, Australian National University Press, Canberra, 1988.

Roe, Michael, 'A Model Aboriginal State', *Aboriginal History*, vol. 10, pt 1, 1986, pp. 40–44.

Stokes, Geoff, 'Citizenship and Aboriginality: Two Conceptions of Identity in Aboriginal Political Thought', in Stokes (ed.), *The Politics of Identity in Australia*, Cambridge University Press, Melbourne, 1997, pp. 158–71.

Williams, John A., *Politics of the New Zealand Maori: Protest and Cooperation, 1891–1909*, Auckland University Press, Auckland, 1969.

Film

Morgan, Alec (dir.), Lousy Little Sixpence, Ronin Films, Canberra, 1982.

Theses

Barwick, Diane, 'A Little More Than Kin': Regional Affiliation and Group Identity Among Aboriginal Migrants in Melbourne, PhD, Australian National University, 1963.

Goodall, Heather, A History of Aboriginal Communities in New South Wales, 1909–1939, PhD, University of Sydney, 1982.

Matthews, Patricia, 'Uplifting Our Aboriginal People': The Victorian Aboriginal Group, 1930–1971, BA Hons, Department of History, Monash University, 1985.

Penney, Jan, Encounters on the River: Aborigines and Europeans in the Murray Valley 1820–1920, PhD, La Trobe University, 1989.

Index

Abbott, C.L., 28
Aboriginal affairs, Commonwealth jurisdiction, 19
Aboriginal Fellowship Group, 10
Aboriginal Sunday (Aborigines' Day), 88, 113, 132
Aborigines Assistance Committee, 22, 120
Aborigines' Friends' Association, 86
Aborigines Progressive Association, 1, 7, 9, 21, 23, 82, 108, 112, 114
Aborigines Protection Association, 3, 27
Aborigines Protection Board, New South Wales, 3, 21, 31, 33, 37, 42, 43, 59, 103, 106–08, 114–6, 118–9
Aborigines Protection League, 133
Aborigines' Uplift Society, 110, 113, 121
Aboriginal people and Jewish people, 5–6, 19, 21, 108, 111
Anderson, Joe 8, 36, 131
Anti-Slavery and Aborigines Protection Society, 8, 10, 17, 46, 62, 69, 83
Association for the Protection of Native Races, 8, 10, 17, 22, 53, 103
Austin, Ada, 120, 124
Australian Aboriginal Progressive Association, 1, 7
Australian Aborigines Amelioration Association, 11, 17, 77
Australian Aborigines' League
  authorship of representations and mode of address, 12–13
  constitution, 11–12, 48–51
  formation, 11, 37
  methods, 6–7, 17, 40, 59, 62, 69, 84, 87, 91, 115, 122, 126
  motto, 14, 70, 101
  names for organisation, 11–12
  petition to King George V(I), 7–10, 17–20, 35–41, 45, 53, 73–5, 77–8, 80–82, 84, 97, 101, 122, 124, 128–9
  programme, 13–14, 49–50, 65–6, 78
  relationship with non-Aboriginal members and organisations, 10–13, 17–18, 48, 53
  significance, 1
  standing, 18

Australian Aborigines' League, and
  Aboriginal rights, 9, 13–14, 24, 55
Aboriginal state, 9–10, 80, 113
Aboriginality, 15, 34, 49, 51–3, 58, 67–8, 74–6, 100, 109
'aliens' (and other non-British migrants), 14, 57, 59, 63, 69, 72, 82, 90, 101, 111, 113, 122–4
anthropology and anthropologists, 17, 30, 32–4, 41, 93, 103, 114, 127–8, 133–4
absorption and assimilation, 74, 117
birthright (status as original owners), 6, 20, 27, 29–30, 36, 47, 55, 58, 62, 64, 73–4, 79, 90–94, 101, 109, 123, 127
Board for the Protection of Aborigines, Victoria, 35, 37, 119–21
Britishness and British justice, 14, 43, 90–91, 104, 114–15, 119, 124
capacity of Aborigines, 30, 33, 39, 56, 58–9, 62–3, 67–8, 75–6, 80, 84, 90
Christians and Christianity, 38, 43–4, 79, 85, 92, 96
citizenship and citizenship rights, 6–7, 9, 13–14, 22–4, 28, 33, 39, 43–4, 51–2, 55, 57, 59, 72–3, 78, 94, 99, 103–5, 108, 111, 123
commemoration, 20, 27, 66, 72, 82, 86, 88
compensation, 10, 14, 30, 94, 109, 113, 128
conditions, 16, 37, 42–3, 51, 71, 83, 98–100, 114
'day of mourning', 19–20, 82, 87–8
disease and depopulation, 30, 38, 63, 66, 69, 85, 93, 107–8, 116, 128
dispossession, 10, 14–15, 23, 27–9, 31, 33, 36, 41–3, 55, 58, 83, 92, 94, 112–13, 116, 120, 123, 128–9
duty of the Crown and colonisers, 10, 27, 34, 38–9, 43–4, 51, 70, 94, 110, 129
education and training, 28, 31, 39, 43–5, 47–50, 52, 57, 60, 65–6, 74, 78–80, 84, 89, 96, 98, 104, 108, 116, 123, 126, 129
employment and unemployment, 30, 47, 49–50, 56, 76, 90, 94, 98, 100, 115–16
expulsion, 15–16, 42, 59, 65
extermination, 32, 34, 79–80, 104, 110, 128
extinction, 31–2, 34–7, 44, 93–4

Australian Aborigines' League, and (*cont.*)
federal government control or responsibility, 16, 31, 33, 44, 46, 54–5, 64–5, 75, 80–81, 84–5, 93–4, 96, 98–9, 122–3
federal (or national) government policy, 6, 44, 49, 54, 65, 68, 73–7, 81, 113–14, 117, 121, 124, 126
franchise, 50, 94, 97–8, 101, 122–3, 129
frontier violence, 15, 22, 28, 32, 34, 43, 45, 62, 66–7, 70, 76, 79–80, 83, 91–2, 96, 115
governance, 15–16, 21–2, 31, 33, 42–3, 45, 49–50, 57, 59, 65, 72, 81, 96, 100, 103–4, 106–7, 114–16, 118–19, 126
history of Australia, 30, 34, 46, 51, 55, 58, 62, 76, 79, 88, 91–2, 94, 96; *see also* history, biblical
Hitler and Nazi Germany, 23, 100, 108, 111, 115, 128
housing, 50, 84–6, 107, 116
indigenous peoples and indigenous/black policy (non-Australian), 33, 36, 41, 44, 60–61, 74, 76, 80–81, 97; *see also* Maori
kinship, 8, 13, 36
labour movement, 99–100, 104
land development, 16, 31, 42, 49–50, 54, 59–61, 64, 66, 71–2, 76–7, 79, 82, 89–90, 101, 104–5, 116, 120
land grants, 7, 27, 31, 45, 50, 57, 63–4, 66
law, 49, 54, 66, 78, 81; *see also* governance
Magna Carta, 6, 81, 110, 122, 124
malnutrition, 47, 63, 111, 114, 116
marriage, 98, 100
memory, 6, 15–16, 22, 66–7, 70, 80, 115; *see also* history of Australia
military service, 22–3, 34, 51, 92, 112–13
missionaries and missions, 28–30, 32, 34, 37–9, 57, 76, 112, 117
monarchy, 7–8, 27, 35–6, 57, 69, 74, 77, 79–80, 94, 103, 112, 127
parliamentary representation, 7–9, 29, 31, 33, 35–6, 40–41, 44–6, 52, 54, 60, 64, 73–4, 76, 81–2, 94, 101–2, 114, 122–2, 124, 126, 128–9
pensions (and other allowances), 50, 57, 59, 63, 65–6, 78, 102, 110–11, 116, 120–4
police, 28, 31, 33–4, 39, 42, 45, 83–4, 91, 96
poverty, 30, 56, 74
protection and protectors, 28, 31–2, 39, 44, 91–3, 101, 110, 126, 128
protection boards, 16, 31, 33, 37, 39, 42, 100, 116–17
racial discrimination, 13, 23, 29–30, 32, 35, 47, 49, 52, 55, 58, 62–3, 65, 67, 73, 81, 93, 97–9, 102, 109–10, 113, 116–17, 124
racial equality, 38, 74, 96, 98

Australian Aborigines' League, and (*cont.*)
racial minorities, 20–21, 23, 103–4, 118, 121, 124, 128–9; *see also* Aboriginal people and Jewish people
racism, 13–14, 32, 36, 51–2, 56–8, 62, 74, 83, 92–3, 96, 98, 101
rations, 30, 43, 47, 49–50, 57, 59, 65, 69, 78, 82, 84, 98, 107, 115–16, 119–20, 128
removal of children, 22, 31, 47–8, 117
reserves, 16, 22, 31, 34, 42–3, 49–50, 54, 56–7, 59, 64, 66, 78, 89, 101–2, 104, 127–9
rights to land, *see* birthright (status of original owners)
segregation, 18, 83, 134
sexual abuse, 43, 68–9, 83
theory of progress, 13–14
'thinking black', 8, 67, 73, 75, 90, 93, 101, 109–10, 129, 132
'uplift', 7, 13–14, 28, 49, 52, 54, 56–8, 60, 62, 64, 67–9, 72, 75–6, 80, 88–90, 94, 101, 104
white Australia, 43, 66–7, 90, 101
Australian National Missionary Council
Australian Natives Association, 20
Australian Workers' Union, 4

Baillie, Helen, 10, 11, 12, 13, 46, 132
Barwick, Diane, 1
Basedow, Herbert, 30, 133
Batman, John (and treaty), 19–20, 52, 66, 70, 72, 110, 113, 132
Bennett, Mary, 8, 11
black power, 24
Bleakley, J.W., 29, 39
Briggs, Hylus, 132
Brown, Amy, 17
Burdeu, Arthur, 11–13, 18, 22–3, 53, 82, 104–6, 113, 118–121, 131–2; *see also* Australian Aborigines' League
Burraga, King; *see* Anderson, Joe

Chanter, J.M., 27
children, removal from parents, 22; *see also* Australian Aborigines League and removal of children
Chinnery, E.W.P., 117, 127–8
Christianity, 5, 11; *see also* Australian Aborigines' League and Christians and Christianity; humanitarians and humanitarianism; missionaries
Church of Christ, 11
Communist Party of Australia, 22, 116–17
Cooper, Ada, 6
Cooper, Lynch, 52, 132

Cooper, William; see also Australian Aborigines' League,
  authority as leader, 4
  birth, childhood and youth, 2–3, 126
  children, 3, 23
  Christianity, 2–3, 5–6, 125, 127
  death, 4, 23
  education, 5, 11, 38, 78
  expulsion from reserve, 3
  historical status, 1
  health, 22
  historical sources, 2, 130
  inspiration for later leaders, 24
  land grants, 27
  marriages, 3–4
  move to Melbourne, 4, 130
  petitioning, 27
  poverty, 4–5, 11, 127
  work, 3–5, 44–5, 78
Cootamundra Girls Home, 48
Coranderrk, 3, 4, 7, 15, 39
Council for Civil Liberties, 108
Cumeroogunga, 3, 4, 11, 15–16, 21, 29, 31, 42, 47, 60–61, 64, 71–2, 77, 85, 98, 102, 106, 108, 114, 116–19, 125–6, 130
  walk–off, 17, 22, 114–20
Curtin, John, 23

Danvers, J.G., 21, 71
Davidson, Mark, 118–19
Day of Mourning, 18, 82, 86–8
disease and depopulation, 2
Duren, Jane, 7

Elkin, Professor A.P., 10

Ferguson, William, 9, 19, 82, 132
Framlingham, 121
frontier violence, 2, 134

Goodall, Heather, 7, 131
Gribble, Rev. Ernest, 11, 37–9, 41–2, 46
Gribble, Rev. John, 3
Gsell, Mons., 70

Hamilton, Agnes, 3
Harris, John, 46, 62–4, 69–70, 83–4
Harris, Norman, 40
history, biblical, 5–6, 19, 61, 67, 95
humanitarians and humanitarianism, 5, 10–11, 17, 132

James, Shadrach, 6, 8, 10, 16, 20, 28, 32, 43–5, 132; see also Australian Aborigines' League
James, Thomas, 6

Jewish Holocaust Museum and Research Centre, 133

Kitson, W. H., 112
Kramer, E. E., 89
Kulin, 15, 20

Lake Tyers, 37
Lyons, Joseph A., 19, 36–7, 40–41, 54, 64–6, 70, 73, 77, 80–81, 87, 90–97, 102–3, 113–14, 124

McEwen, John, 23, 86–7, 89–90, 101–2, 104–6, 109–13, 117–18, 127, 133–34
McGregor, Russell, 7
McQuiggan, Arthur, 21–22, 106–7, 114
McQuiggan, Mrs, 106–7, 114
Makin, H., 39
Maloga, 2–3, 5–7, 27, 125, 127
Maloney, W.,
Mannix, Archbishop Daniel, 10
Maori, 8, 35, 41, 44, 60, 63, 67, 76, 81, 94, 113, 122
Matthews, Daniel, 2–3, 5–6, 125, 134
Matthews, Janet, 2, 125, 134
Menzies, Robert, 121–4, 127–9
missionaries, 2–3, 5, 14; see also Australian Aborigines' League and missionaries and missions
model Aboriginal state, 9–10
Morgan, Anna, 16, 42–4, 111
Morgan, Caleb, 42, 132
Morley, N.M., 11, 51
Morley, Rev. William, 22, 53–4, 103
Morrell, S., 134
Murray, Hubert, 44
Murrie, Annie Clarendon, 3
music, 5, 52, 72, 125, 133

Native Union, 1
Nelson, Sarah, 4
Neville, A.O., 103–4, 117
New Zealand, 7
Nicholls, Douglas, 24, 44, 52, 82, 113, 122–4, 129, 132
Noble, Rev. James, 38, 40, 110
Norman, W.A., 125

Old Pioneers Memorial Fund, 19, 72
Onus, Bill, 23–4
Onus, Eric, 22, 24
O'Shannassy, John, 2, 78
Palm Island, 79
Parker, A.E., 39

Paterson, Thomas, 43–6, 52–7, 67–9, 73–7, 87, 95–6, 113
Patten, George, 22, 119
Patten, John, 18, 21–3, 108, 112, 114
Perkins, J.A., 40

Queen Victoria, 7–8, 27, 127

racial discrimination, 4–5; *see also* Australian Aborigines' League
racism, 21; *see also* Australian Aborigines' League
reserves, 21; *see also* Coranderrk, Cumeroogunga, Framlingham, Maloga, Palm Island, Warangesda
rights, 1, 9; *see also* Australian Aborigines' League and Aboriginal rights; Australian Aborigines' League and citizenship and citizenship rights
Russell, W., 39

Schenck, Rev. R.S., 34
Selby, Isaac, 19–20, 66, 70, 72, 132
self-determination, *see* Australian Aborigines' League and governance
Sexton, Rev. J.H., 86
Smith, Claude, 66

Smithers, Ernest, 106
South Africa, 7
Spencer, Baldwin, 33, 134
Stephenson, P.R., 18
Stevens, Bertram, 18, 47–8, 58–61, 70–2, 85–6, 98–9, 114–16, 118
Stewart, Fred, 102
Strehlow, T.G.H., 114

Tamwoy, Jomen, 125
Taylor, W., 40
Thomson, Donald, 17, 41, 133
trade unions, 11, 97
Tucker, Margaret, 4, 22, 52, 116, 132
Tuckiar case, 54
Turnbull, Clive, 13, 78

Unaipon, David, 18, 86–8, 110, 122

Victorian Aboriginal Group, 10, 17
Victorian Tribal Council, 24

Warangesda, 2
Wright, Tom, 17

Yorta Yorta, 1–3, 5–7, 15, 24; *see also* Cumeroogunga; Maloga